ALABAM

Portrait of a Stat

ALABAMA
Portrait of a State

Color Photography by Dan Brothers
History by Wayne Greenhaw

Black Belt Press
Montgomery

Black Belt Press
P.O. Box 551
Montgomery, AL 36101

Library of Congress Cataloging-in-Publication Data is available.
ISBN 1-881320-39-1

Design by Steve Garst and Karen Martin.
Illustrations by Steve Garst.

Printed in Italy by Milanostampa.

On the cover: mouth of Little River Canyon, Cherokee County.
Right, Spring Falls in Rock Bridge Canyon, Franklin County.
Overleaf, Gulf State Park fishing pier.

 The Black Belt, defined by its dark, rich soil, stretches across central Alabama. It was the heart of the cotton belt. It was and is a place of great beauty, of extreme wealth and grinding poverty, of pain and joy. Here we take our stand, listening to the past, looking to the future.

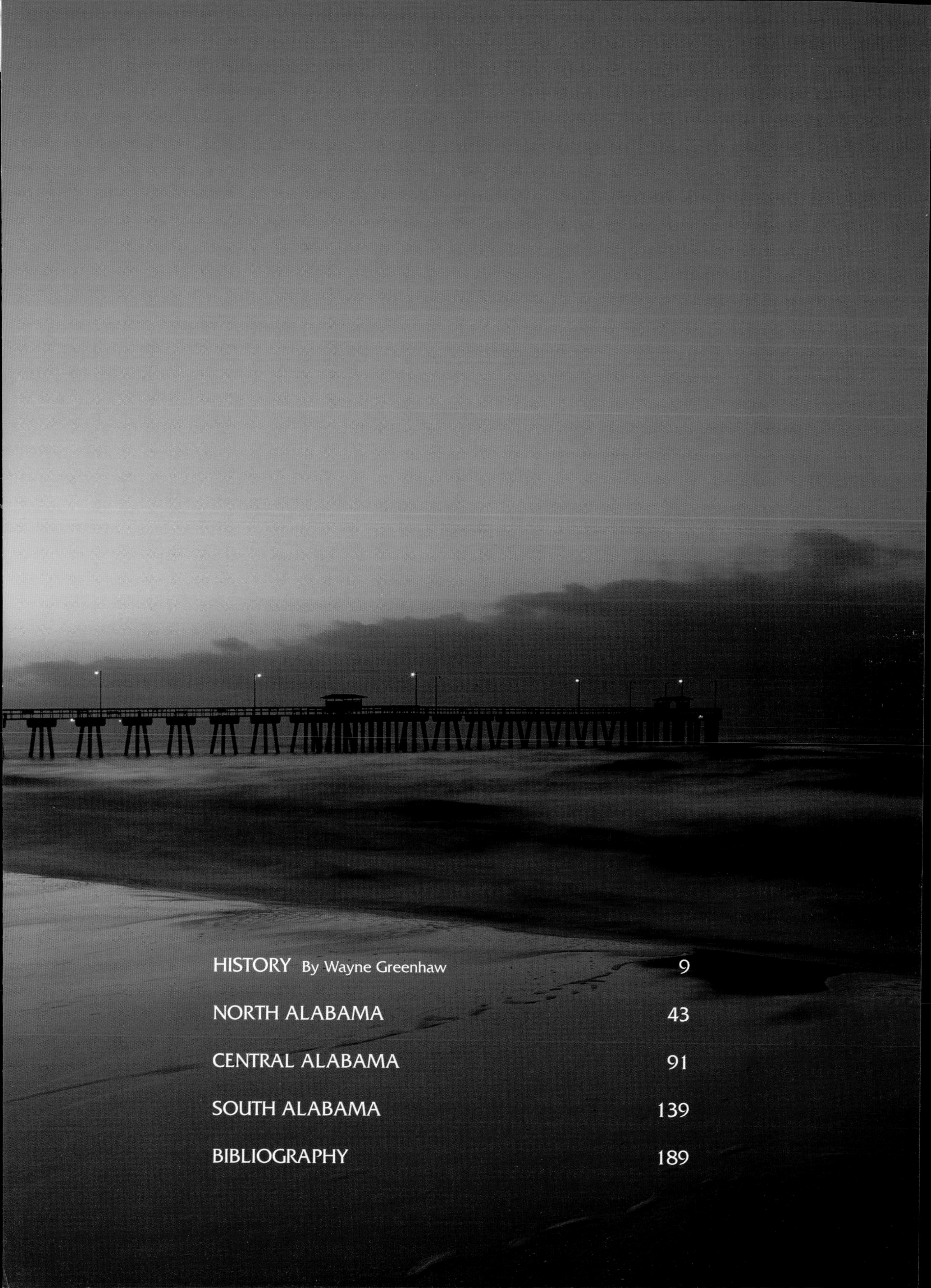

HISTORY

By Wayne Greenhaw

Alabama's history is rich with tales of larger-than-life individuals, from Prince Madoc of Wales, who might have been the first European explorer to set foot in the territory, long before Christopher Columbus, to Governor Big Jim Folsom, who once lined up a dozen Radio City Music Hall dancers and proceeded to kiss each one, thereby earning him the nickname in the northern press as "Kissing Jim."

It is not without some foundation that Madoc, a twelfth century prince from the British province of Wales, landed on the Gulf coast in the year 1170, possibly on the shore of Mobile Bay, and led a band of Welshmen as far north as present-day Elmore County, where Welsh-type mining shafts were found as late as 1964.

However, the first European country to claim title to the land later to be known as Alabama was Spain, within ten years after Columbus made his initial discovery. It was in 1540 that Hernando de Soto landed on the Florida coast and moved northward into the Alabama territory. The state received its name from the tribe of Indians, the Alabamu, who inhabited much of the land of central Alabama when de Soto and his men zigzagged north and west.

Twenty years later, Tristan de Luna led an expedition in an attempt to find the provinces of Tascaluza and Coosa which de Soto had described in such detail. The explorer's men occupied a village on the eastern shore of Mobile Bay, but storms and starvation proved too much of a hardship for them.

By the next century, it was discovered that Alabama was occupied by four Indian nations, Cherokee, Choctaw, Chickasaw, and Creek. In 1699, the French, led by Pierre Le Moyne d'Iberville and Jean-Baptiste Le Moyne de Bienville, moved onto Dauphin Island, where they found sixty skeletons in the sand dunes. Others followed, but it was Iberville who chose the spot near present-day Mobile for the first major fort in the area, Fort Louis, named for King Louis XIV.

It was in 1704 that the ship *Pelican* arrived bringing supplies, soldiers, and young women. Iberville himself had asked the Paris government for a hundred "young and well-bred" girls to be sent to marry the French Canadian settlers and soldiers. The girls were selected by the Bishop of Quebec from orphanages and convents. After yellow fever ran rampant through the ship following a stop in Havana, a number died. Finally, the *Pelican* arrived with twenty-three "virtuous maidens" and two chaperones. Gaunt and some feverish, they were housed in primitive quarters and given cornbread to eat. They rebelled, having

Sequoyah, who lived for a while in northeast Alabama and traveled extensively through the territory, invented an alphabet with 85 symbols of the Cherokee language. This made the Cherokees the only tribe in America to have a written language.

been accustomed to French bread, and what was termed the Petticoat Insurrection took place before weddings helped them accept their new home. The French continued to send women, and as late as 1728 they were known as cassette girls because they brought their possessions in small trunks called *cassettes.*

The New Territory

By 1798, Alabama was part of the Mississippi Territory. In 1817, the Alabama Territory was formed after the survey by Andrew Ellicott was completed. During this time, a few whites, like Scotsman Alexander McGillivray, whose father had been a young indentured servant, befriended the Indians and married into the tribes. McGillivray married Sehoy, a Creek princess of the Wind clan, and through their marriage his political clout among the Creeks heightened considerably.

In 1804, the former vice-president of the United States, Aaron Burr, fatally wounded Alexander Hamilton in a duel at Washington, D.C. After he was caught and jailed in Natchez, he escaped and fled toward Florida. On the night of February 19, 1807, he was arrested near Wakefield in Washington County, north of Mobile. A local lawyer, Nicholas Perkins, spotted Burr and another man riding in the moonlight, summoned the sheriff, and found Burr in the kitchen of a house warming himself. Perkins and the sheriff rode to Fort Stoddard, elicited the help of soldiers, and returned to arrest Burr and transport him to Richmond, Virginia, where he was tried for treason.

During this time in north Alabama, John Hunt built a cabin near Big Springs in 1802. Lands for this and other settlements along the Tennessee River valley were obtained through a treaty with Cherokee Indians in 1805, and Madison County was organized in 1808. A letter to a friend in Virginia from Mrs. Anne Royall, an early visitor, stated that "the land around Huntsville, and the whole of Madison County . . . is rich and beautiful as you can imagine, and the appearance of wealth would baffle belief."

Mooresville, only a few miles to the west, became a thriving river town and, within a few years, became the first incorporated municipality in the new state. As early as 1816, the tavern at Mooresville was built by Llewelyn Jones, a soldier of the Revolution who received a federal grant of several sections of land on the river. By 1819 it was a stop on the post road for mail to and from Huntsville. Three years later it was a stop for stagecoaches from Huntsville to Russellville across the Tennessee River Valley. Visitors found a cheerful fire in the fireplace of the main room, with a clock on the hand-carved mantel, and a newspaper usually several weeks old. Two rooms on the second floor were normally shared by several travelers. With the evening meal, a glass of wine or liquor was usually served. Ice for his drink was found in an icehouse a few feet from the backdoor. Ice was chiseled from the frozen river in the dead of winter and kept in the icehouse all year long. All of this for a cost of a half-dollar plus corn for the horse at fifty cents a bushel or six-and-one-half cents for three bundles of fodder.

Bonapartists from France colonized Demopolis in 1818 and began planting vineyards for grapes to make wine and olive trees for oil along the Tombigbee River. The U.S. Congress granted almost 100,000 acres for this effort.

Indian Troubles

In the first years after Europeans arrived in the territory, Indians were stirred to violent action by the fiery oratory of the great Shawnee chief Tecumseh, who came south and traveled among the Cherokees in northeast Alabama and the Creeks through central Alabama. With their bodies painted black and scowls painted on their faces, Tecumseh's group "looked like a procession of devils." Tecumseh's eyes burned with a "supernatural lustre" when he urged war against the white settlers.

There were numerous skirmishes between the Indians and white soldiers, until one morning in August in 1812, Indians were spotted near Fort Mims, located a day's hard ride on horseback north of Mobile. Brigadier General Ferdinand L. Claiborne of the Mississippi territorial militia was visiting Major Daniel Beasley, a Mississippi lawyer who was given command of the fort in south Alabama, late in July when he remarked that the fort was "exceedingly exposed" and ordered Beasley to "enroll every citizen that is willing to perform duty" to build two additional blockhouses, strengthen pickets, keep scouts

At Horseshoe Bend in Tallapoosa County, Andrew Jackson led volunteer troops against the once-powerful Creek nation. In March of 1814, more than a thousand Creeks under the command of Chief Menawa fought valiantly, but by the end of the day more than 500 Creeks lay dead or dying and another 300 were shot while trying to escape across the Tallapoosa River. Among the white troops wounded that day was 21-year-old Tennessee volunteer Sam Houston.

on the move throughout the area to watch out for unfriendly Creeks, and to respect their enemy. On the morning of the 13th of August, Beasley wrote Claiborne that two slave boys had given a "false alarm," saying "a great number of Indians painted, running, and hallooing" and that they also reported Indians taking over a nearby plantation and were "committing every kind of havoc."

Just before the attack, James Cornells rode to the gate and shouted a warning, saying William Weatherford, the dreaded Creek Chief Red Eagle, was on his way with a band of warriors. Instead of heeding, Beasley ordered Cornells arrested. Cornells fled on horseback. At the time he left, sand was piled so high next to the door of the fort, the gates could not close.

As lunch was being served in the fort, shortly after noon on August 30th, Indians rushed through the open gate. According to John Ehle's *Trail of Tears,* "in the sweltering heat of Alabama, one thousand Red Stick warriors, accompanied by many shamans, their sticks red and waving, their faces painted black, their war bonnets flashing color, their throats hoarse from feverish cries, attacked U.S. Fort Mims." Although Weatherford had implored them not to kill women and children, within the next hours at least 250 people, and by some accounts as many as 553—men, women, and children—were massacred or taken as slaves. Less than 100 attacking Indians were killed. "The corpses were scalped and in other ways mutilated, left for dogs and buzzards,

This marker was erected at the site of Fort Toulouse, built by the French in 1717 as an outpost for fur trade with the Indians. Near here the Coosa and Tallapoosa rivers join to form the Alabama River. At this spot, Chief Red Eagle, also known as William Weatherford, surrendered to General Andrew Jackson in the aftermath of the battle of Horseshoe Bend, ending the Creek Indian War. The fort has been excavated and is being rebuilt.

exposed to rot in the Alabama sun," Ehle wrote.

The slaughter at Fort Mims rallied Tennessee Governor Willie Blount, who ordered his militia armed and to be led by Major General Andrew Jackson, who marched southward, established several forts, and went about the systematic defeat of the Indians. Finally, with William McIntosh and Big Warrior leading friendly Creeks, the militia bottled the militant Creeks in a bend of Tallapoosa River called the Horseshoe. On March 27, 1814, "arrows, and spears, and balls were flying; swords and tomahawks were gleaming in the sun; and the whole peninsula rang with the yell of the savage, and the groans of the dying." By night, the Tallapoosa was a river of blood. The Creek nation had fallen. Within weeks, Chief Red Eagle, who had not been at Horseshoe Bend, rode into Fort Jackson at the confluence of the Coosa and Tallapoosa rivers. Old Fort

Toulouse had been renamed for the commanding general. Weatherford surrendered, and the Treaty of Fort Jackson was signed, giving the U.S. nearly half the land which would five years later become the state.

Alabama Fever

The *Alabama* was the first steamboat constructed in this industrial as well as agricultural region when it was built at St. Stephens in 1818. However, its engines were not powerful enough to push against the strong currents in the state's rivers. The following year more powerful steamboats appeared on the Tombigbee as far north as Demopolis, picking up cotton grown throughout the Black Belt to be shipped out of the port of Mobile for England and New England textile plants.

In June of 1819, President James Monroe, who three months earlier had signed an act enabling Alabama to become a state, arrived at the assembly hall where the state constitutional convention was to be held. After a dinner with 100 citizens, 21 toasts, the discharge of cannons and songs sung, the convention elected John Williams Baker its president and John Campbell its secretary. On August 2, after discussing all the issues of the day, the constitution was adopted but never submitted to the people for ratification.

The new land caused the Alabama fever to sweep the large cities of the seaboard from Savannah to Boston. A lawyer named Andrew Dexter left his practice in Boston to come south and become a land-speculator. He had already proven to be the adventurous sort and had gone to Nova Scotia a few years earlier to try the same entrepreneurship but was caught with a married woman and forced to leave. Now he eyed the land on the high bluffs of the Alabama River. Abner McGehee saw possibilities of speculation in land that was said to be rich in ore and other minerals near Elyton close to what was to become Birmingham in the last half of the nineteenth century. Presbyterian ministers became interested in the area around Muscle Shoals on the Tennessee River in northwest Alabama. And farmers from South and North Carolina, Virginia, Georgia, and Tennessee signed with the land office at Milledgeville to homestead the Alabama frontier.

In June of 1819, representatives from throughout the Alabama Territory met in Huntsville for the constitutional convention to form the state. U.S. President James Monroe was greeted by Clement C. Clay, who had come to Huntsville eight years earlier. He had practiced law, farmed, and joined with General Jackson to fight the Indians. He was a member of the territorial legislature. During the convention, he was named chairman of a commission with the responsibility of writing the state's first laws and constitution. At a public dinner at the Green Bottom Inn, one of Alabama's first hostelries, Clay praised President Monroe, who along with two cabinet members stayed at the Inn where, in December of 1819, General Jackson made his headquarters. The owner of the Green Bottom, John Connelly, loved to race horses, and Jackson brought with him "some of his horses and roosters for a few days rest."

The First Governor

William Wyatt Bibb, who had been territorial governor, was inaugurated the state's first governor. Born in Virginia, Bibb presided over the territory from its capital at St. Stephens in south Alabama north of Mobile. He concerned himself with developing education, transportation, and a new banking system. In the first election after the constitutional convention, Bibb ran against Marmaduke Williams of Tuscaloosa, a former congressman from North Carolina. In this election, the two sides that squared off were the Georgia faction, of which Bibb was leader, and the North Carolina faction, which picked Williams to represent it. Out of a total of 15,482 votes, Bibb won by a 1,202 margin. Bibb reigned over the temporary capital in Huntsville. In July of 1820, after he had served little more than six months, Bibb fell from the back of his horse while riding on his Coosada plantation. Bedridden, he died a few days later and his brother, Thomas Wyatt Bibb, a merchant, planter, and legislator, was appointed to serve out the remainder of his brother's term, until November of 1821.

William Wyatt Bibb, who had been governor of the Alabama territory, was elected the state's first governor by the General Assembly of fifty-one representatives and twenty-two senators. Bibb, who was from Coosada north of Montgomery, spoke openly in favor of the first state capitol being located at Cahaba at the confluence of the Alabama and Cahaba rivers. Bibb died in 1820 after a fall from his horse that bruised his kidney.

The Alabama constitution, written by Clay and his committee members, was a liberal document for its time, establishing universal white manhood voting rights without property, tax-paying, or militia requirements. It also allowed similar liberal options for officeholders. The governor would be elected by the people, not the legislature, and the basis for apportionment was white. Its bill of rights section did not dictate any belief in God, as many of the other states' did. Although slavery was legal, it required that slave-owners treat them "with humanity" and "necessary food and clothing" and stated that owners were "to abstain from all injuries to them extending to life and limb." Few Southern states had such requirements. It went a step further: making the punishment for killing a slave the same as the offense "committed on a free white person," with a clause stating that killing a slave during an insurrection was justified. Thomas Bibb and Israel Pickens tried to give legislature the power to enfranchise free blacks, but this move was defeated. The document was adopted on August 2, 1819, but it never went to the people for a vote of ratification.

Soon after he took office, Bibb urged the legislature to elect

Alabama's two senators. Chosen by the Georgia faction were John Williams Walker from the north and Charles Tait from the south. Walker served three years as Senator. A health problem forced his resignation and retirement in Alabama. However, leading the North Carolina faction were state senators from the Black Belt of south Alabama who supported William Rufus King of Selma. They stated emphatically that Tait had not been a resident of the area long enough to represent it. King had served in the North Carolina state legislature and in the U.S. House of Representatives from that state for three terms. He had also represented the U.S. in negotiations with European countries prior to his moving to Dallas County, where he purchased a plantation and a home he called King's Bend on the Alabama River. A politician of superb talent, he represented Alabama in the U.S. Senate for twenty-nine years before he became vice-president in 1852 and died of fever shortly after being sworn into office in Cuba. Not only was he Alabama's highest officeholder, he was the only vice-president ever to be sworn in on foreign soil. He died at his beloved home in Alabama several months later.

Thomas Bibb, a landowner, merchant, and planter from Belle Mina in Limestone County, president of the state senate, when his older brother, Governor William Wyatt Bibb, died in office. Thomas served out his brother's term but never had the popularity enjoyed by his brother, and south Alabama legislators did not approve his run for re-election. Instead, they elected Israel Pickens, a former congressman from North Carolina who moved to the Alabama territory as register of the land office at St. Stephens.

Soon the legislature voted to house the first capital of the new state in Cahaba on the Alabama River south of Selma. It was not long before the town received horrendous downpours, flooding its streets in 1821 and 1822. The flooding was followed by an outbreak of yellow fever when mosquitoes bred in the muddy moisture that turned rancid in the tropical-like heat of the summer.

When the legislature met in the fall of 1821 in the town mortified by disease, as rains fell in torrents, Governor Thomas Bibb also outlined a depressing picture of the state's condition: the treasury was empty, currency problems were outstanding, debt was heavy, and the sale of lands which had been put aside to support a state university was imminent. He then turned the affairs of state over to the new governor, Israel Pickens. A North Carolina faction leader from Washington County, he later moved to Greene and Hale counties. A native of North Carolina, he was the first of that group to be elected and inaugurated governor.

Two years later he ran for re-election against Henry Chambers, one of the Georgia faction leaders of the Royal party, who had opposed him the first time. Pickens's defeat of Chambers marked the first real strength of the Black Belt in Alabama politics. Its influence would dominate the state for a long time. Pickens's supporters also won control of both the House and the Senate, thereby con-

Senator Clement Comer Clay was a Huntsville banker and attorney. Born in Virginia, his family moved to Tennessee, where he read law. He moved to Madison County in 1811, served in the Alabama militia in the Creek Indian War, was a stockholder in the Planters and Merchants Bank, and played an important role in writing the constitution. Elected chief justice of the Alabama Supreme Court and then to Congress, he became governor in 1836.

trolling executive and legislative branches of government. With his power, Pickens turned the state around, strengthened the monetary system by creating the Bank of Alabama, and provided a means for cotton farmers to be financed and make better-than-decent profits.

Lafayette Visits

In 1825, the French hero of the American revolution, the Marquis de Lafayette, visited the state. On the last day of March a party of the most important leaders of Montgomery was sent to Fort Mitchell on the Chattahoochee River to welcome the old soldier. Among these was Thomas S. Woodward, the oldest brigadier general in Alabama. "In a very impressive manner," Woodward recalled later in his *Reminiscences*, Bolling Hall, a former U.S. representative from Montgomery, welcomed Lafayette to the state.

On the evening of April 2, the group was greeted at Lucas Tavern on the Federal Road near Mount Meigs. Walter B. Lucas's place "was done up better than it will ever be again," wrote Woodward. Plantation owners lined the columned front porch and shook the hand of the Frenchman, who was given supper and a private bedroom.

Following breakfast on Sunday morning, April 3, Lafayette was accompanied into Montgomery by the large contingent. "Such a cavalcade never traveled that road before or since," Woodward remembered.

In Montgomery, church sermons were suspended and most of the population gathered on Andrew Dexter's Goat Hill, the highest hill on the eastern edge of town. As the traveling party came into sight, the crowd of almost 2,000 began their applause. Not only did nearly every soul in Montgomery show up for the welcoming, several hundred from the surrounding countryside rode in for the occasion and a group of dignitaries from the capital at Cahaba traveled to Montgomery by riverboat. The travelers stopped their carriages and dismounted their horses on a sand flat several hundred yards east of the hill. They formed a column and marched with Lafayette in the lead to the top of the hill, where the city's band played "Hail to the Chief." The applause crescendoed until Colonel Bolling Hall raised his hands.

After welcoming the Frenchman in verbose and poetic language, Colonel Hall turned the podium over to Governor Pickens, whose job it was to introduce Lafayette. While the lengthy introduction continued, a number of local citizens passed jugs of the finest whiskey made in the area. By the time the governor finished, there were shouts of "Amen, brother!" and "Yea! Yea! Yea, sir!"

When the marquis finally spoke, thanking all of those who had come to hear him and meet him, Captain John Carr, an elderly Irish veteran of the Revolutionary War, raised his hands to shout his happiness, fell back and disappeared down a well. While fellow townspeople lowered a rope to pull him out, General Lafayette never missed a word of his speech.

Later, the party paraded down Market Street to Court Square and Commerce Street to the home of prominent citizen John Edmondson, where the famous French soldier-statesman greeted the throng in the parlor.

On the following day, Lafayette met with Montgomery men of substance who had also fought in the revolution. That afternoon, once again a number of prominent citizens crowded into the Edmondson parlor to speak with, touch, or simply see the famous man. On the evening of April 4, all the leaders and their families were invited to a ball in honor of Lafayette on the second floor of Freeney's Tavern. Late that night, Governor Pickens and his entourage escorted Lafayette aboard the paddlewheel steamer that had brought them to Montgomery. The entire party proceeded to the capital at Cahaba.

Writing of life on the frontier of 1830, A. E. Powell of Tuscaloosa recalled that an "old gentleman from whom Father had rented some land, came to the cabin, at once took in the situation, and spoke words of kindness and encouragement to Mother, told her there was a better time coming, and for her not to give way.

"The old gentleman's cropper soon came up with what was then considered a full outfit of carpenter's tools for a farmer, to wit: a handsaw, auger and draw knife. He told Mother that he would show her how to make an Alabama bedstead. A few heart pine rails, and some old boards filled up the timber bill, and in a very short time he had improvised a bedstead standing on one leg in each corner of the backend of the cabin, and Mother put up her beds. By this time the genuine kindness and pleasant remarks of the man, uncultivated as they were, had produced a happy change in Mother's feelings, and I don't think that I ever saw her in after-life come so near giving up again."

In north Alabama, a planter named James Jackson built a grand mansion in Lauderdale County, near Florence. With columns surrounding all four sides, Forks of Cypress was an imposing site where Andrew Jackson, before and after he became president, brought his famed race horses to compete at James Jackson's private track.

Cotton was king of economic Alabama in these years, and slavery was a strong part of that economy. Every large town, such as Montgomery, Tuscaloosa, Mobile, and Florence, had a slave market where slaves were bought and sold openly. All did not work on the large cotton farms or in plantation homes. In Huntsville's Bell Factory, one of the first textile manufacturing mills in the state, slaves operated a hundred looms and 3,000 spindles. At the Tannehill furnaces, where iron ore was fashioned from the mines of north-central Alabama, slaves did the manual labor. And William L. Gould, a Scottish miner, owned slaves who mined coal.

In 1836, once again the Alabama land-speculation fever spread through the population centers of the eastern seaboard. This time all Cherokee Indians were rounded up, confined at Fort Payne, and then transported or escorted westward to Oklahoma. Word spread rapidly that the Southern frontier was free of violence following the Trail of Tears.

Traveler's Delight

By the later 1840s, plank roads and railroads crisscrossed the state, making transportation better than ever. Steamboats traveled as far north as Montgomery on the Alabama, Tombigbee, and Mobile river system and Tuscaloosa on the Black Warrior. Because the Indians had been removed, ridding the area of apparent danger, and the transportation was made relatively easy, tourism began to show its face as an economic factor. Among the first hotels, along with the Green Bottom at Huntsville and the tavern at Mooresville, was The Palings at Fort Dale in Butler County on the Federal Road. The first tourist destination in the state was without a doubt the Grand Hotel at Point Clear. The Dana House was built here by Caleb Dana and Joe Nelson in 1820. Twenty-seven years later, F. H. Chamberlain, a large landowner in Baldwin County, built the first Point Clear Hotel with lumber brought across the bay from Mobile. A rambling building 100 feet long, it was two-storied with front galleries extending the entire length. The hotel had forty rooms. There were two wharves, one for men, the other for women, because mixed bathing was frowned upon. The dining room in a separate building provided well-cooked meals with fresh venison and vegetables as well as beef and occasional local fish. The third building was called Texas. It was the bar. It too was two-storied with outside stairs leading upstairs. Late in the nineteenth century the main building was demolished in a hurricane. It was rebuilt and used until 1940.

Another of the older hotels was Blount Springs, which had become popular with social leaders of Huntsville by 1825. A weekly stage ran between the two towns. In 1828 several cottages were built near springs that were believed to have recuperative qualities, especially good for rheumatism, dyspepsia, and infection of the bladder and urinary organs. Situated in the Sequatchee Valley, Blount Springs was called Alabama's Fountain of Youth. In 1850, the owner, George Goffe, built a three-story structure overlooking the rural landscape. With forty

Early in the twentieth century, Alabama tourists enjoyed visiting the ruins of the Tannehill Iron Works between Birmingham and Tuscaloosa. The iron works were destroyed by Union raiders in the last days of the Civil War. Today a state park is located at the site and visitors may learn how important the industry was to the war effort in the 1860s.

rooms, the exterior and foundation were built of slate rock. A porch extended across the front. In the basement was a bar called "The Devil's House," where a stronger liquid than sulphur water was served.

In the 1830s, Bailey Springs near Florence and Tuscumbia, just off the stage road to Nashville, became known as a popular spa. By the 1840s visitors came from as far away as St. Louis and Louisville to sample the healthful effects of the water, and by the late 1850s E. G. Ellis spent more than $40,000 building a hotel and a shed over the three springs. The 1858 season from March to December found 1,550 registered guests at the hotel, also famous for its cuisine. In 1860, Bailey Springs was advertised as "the beautiful shades, walks, bowling saloons, both for ladies and gentlemen, billiard tables, bath houses, and shower baths, long needed, are now ready for visitors; together with a large number of well furnished and finished rooms, to say nothing of the accommodations, which will be the very best the country can afford." Each evening a large ballroom came to life with the music of a brass or string band. Among the testimonials for the Springs was that of Joshua Stamps of Rogersville who "came to the springs about 1845, afflicted with dyspepsia. His condition was very low, and life despaired of. He had tried seven physicians, but all to no effect. In four weeks he was restored to health, and it continued good till the last sickness." Colonel Sam Tate, president of the Memphis and Tennessee Railroad, wrote that "your springs exceed any in the world." In the post-bellum era, Bailey Springs continued to be successful until the early 1890s when a university for women was established there, and it finally closed its operations in the 1920s.

By the 1830s, Bladon Springs near the Tombigbee River in Choctaw County became known as "the Saratoga of the South." Its hotel, with great white pillars in its colonnade, large rooms, a huge ballroom, and

Steamboats were a major mode of transportation during the nineteenth century. Here travelers from south Alabama arrive in Selma, where the steamboat picked up cotton from Black Belt plantations to be carried south and then transported around Florida and up the east coast to New England textile mills.

windows overlooking a beautiful valley, was two stories and a full basement, with room for two hundred guests and another one hundred in surrounding cottages. In steamboat days, three trips a week were made from Mobile to Demopolis, each stopping near Bladon Springs, letting off and picking up visitors. A bar in the hotel basement served wine and liquor day or night. The springs had six fountains, recommended for "the cure of gout, rheumatics, scrofula, skin disease, dyspepsia, diseases incident to females, dropsy, and general debility." Its owner, James Conner, advertised, "For the sportsman there is abundant amusement during fall and winter months. Deer are killed within a mile of the Springs. Foxes are plentiful, and a fine pack of hounds is kept in immediate vicinity. Wild duck and smaller game in abundance."

In the 1820s, the Cedar Hotel was opened at Valhermoso, meaning "Vale of Beauty," near Hartselle in Morgan County. The white sulphur water of the springs was offered from a dipper to cure guests of rheumatism, constipation, diseases of the kidneys, stomach, skin, and liver, nervous prostration and sleeplessness, consumption, and even the distress of gray hair. The three-story building with wide front porches on the first and second floor had eight guest rooms, lobby, parlor, bar, dining room, and a ballroom on the third floor. Cottages around the main building could accommodate six families each. Among its most famous guests were William Rufus King, Julia Tutwiler, and numerous families from England, Switzerland, and Scotland. The hotel was bought by Jean Joseph Giers in 1855. A friend of President Abraham Lincoln, Giers did not believe in slavery, and spent each winter in Washington, D.C., returning to Valhermoso each summer. His wife, however, was a true Southerner and during the Civil War hid Confederate soldiers on the third floor of the hotel when federal troops bivouacked nearby. Their family operated the hotel until 1920.

After Major Charles Lewin came to Tuscaloosa in 1818, he built a fine brick hotel on a ridge high above the Black Warrior River. When the legislature moved the state's capitol to Tuscaloosa in 1826, the 133 members were scattered between six hotels. At least one-fourth stayed at Lewin's tavern. But the competition was fierce. William Clare operated the Mansion House on Sixth Street, Charles S. Patterson the Lagrange Hotel on Broad, Matthew Duffee the Washington Hall, where the First National Bank was later built, Thomas R. Bolling the Indian Queen on Broad at Twenty-fifth Avenue, and Peter Donaldson the Bell Tavern on University Avenue. Lewin's two-storied tavern had wide pine floors, a kitchen and dining area, and through the years was known as Spanish House, Wilson House, Old French Tavern, French House, Ewing's Tavern, and, erroneously, Duffie's Tavern.

The Southerner

To the many who traveled in and through Alabama, the state's early residents were known, like most Southerners, as independent-minded souls with a strong pride in their homeland. An anonymous writer's letter from Alabama to a friend in the North perhaps stated it best. "The manner of these Southerners differ a good deal from those of their more calculating compatriots, the yankees of the north and east. In many respects the diversity is to the advantage of the former; there is a bold gallant bearing, a frank free cordiality, and a generous, almost boundless hospitality, in the Southern planter, which are pleasing. But the abiding thought that 'the people,' as being the source of law, are therefore above law, which is deep-seated throughout this land of 'free institutions,' is much more frequently made operative in the South than in the North. Here 'every man is his own law-maker and law-breaker, judge, jury, and executioner.'

"The darkest side of the Southerner is his quarrelsomeness, and recklessness of human life. The terrible bowie-knife is ever ready to be drawn, and it *is* drawn and used too, on the slightest provocation. Duels are fought with this horrible weapon, in which the combatants are almost chopped to pieces; or with the no less fatal, but less shocking rifle, perhaps within pistol-distance.

"Slavery, doubtless, helps to brutalize the character, by familiarizing the mind with the infliction of human suffering. If an English butcher is popularly reputed unfit to serve on a jury, an American slave-owner is not less incompetent to appreciate what is due to man. I had intended to give you some particulars of the working of 'the domestic institution,' for I have witnessed some of its horrors; but I will not allow my pen to trace much of this, especially as you may learn it from other sources. I am obliged to be very cautious, not only in expressing any sympathy with the slaves, but even in manifesting anything like curiosity to know their condition, for there is a very stern jealousy of a stranger's interference on these points."

Asking the question, "What will be the end of American slavery?" the letter writer goes on to state, "Slaves are indispensable in Alabama while the present condition endures. A man may have a thousand acres of land, but if he have no slaves to cultivate his cotton and corn, his acres are a mere waste, for free labor is out of the question." He concludes that "the institution is doomed. Its end approaches surely, perhaps swiftly."

The question was being argued almost constantly in the legislative halls in Tuscaloosa until the capital was moved once again to Montgomery in 1847, when the new capitol was built on Goat Hill, which had been set aside more than twenty years earlier by its owner, Andrew Dexter, who predicted even then that one day the capitol would sit on his land. On December 14, 1849, at 1:30 p.m., both houses were in session when a fire broke out. All legislators and bureaucrats fled to safety as flames destroyed the new building within a few hours. Using what was left of the foundation, the capitol was rebuilt and was ready for the regular session in November of 1851.

The Tide is Changing

In the halls of the new state capitol, legislators took sides on the pressing debate of whether the South should secede from the Union if the U.S. declared slavery illegal. The most outspoken orator at home as well as in the Congress, where he served in the House of Representatives, was William Lowndes Yancey. Born in Georgia in 1814, he was tall, round-faced, with sunken dark eyes and deep brown hair cut over his ears in the style of the day. He was given to wearing knee-length waistcoats and big floppy bowties that gave him the appearance of a knowledgeable scholar. He at first settled on a plantation near Cahaba, editing the Cahaba *Democrat,* but after many of his slaves were poisoned following a feud between his overseer and another from a neighboring plantation, he sold out and moved to Wetumpka, where he became editor and publisher of the *Argus.* As such, he used printer's ink to further his views. He was elected to the Alabama House of Representatives, then to the State Senate, and later to Congress on the platform of "a strict and rigid construction of the federal Constitution."

Through the years of his political career, Yancey developed his style and his mission. In 1848, Yancey worked to control the Democratic party rather than attempt to form a Southern party. He insisted that protection of the South could be accomplished more successfully through the national party. His Alabama Platform stated that the federal government had a constitutional obligation to protect slave property in the territories. The state Democrats followed his leadership.

Eight years later Yancey took to the stump in support of James Buchanan. In north Alabama he explained that the presidential election was significant. He alerted the people of the Tennessee River Valley, where the majority were moderates and Unionists, that the Republican party was growing stronger and stronger. He warned that if Republicans took power there would be no compromise and they would not work with the South and its leaders. This was the first time the inhabitants of north Alabama had heard the south Alabama viewpoint, and it was stated with clarity.

At the Southern Commercial Convention in Montgomery two years later, Yancey spoke in favor of resuming trade with Africa, and he put the convention on notice with an open discussion of Southern rights and secession. Yancey met with numerous delegates in one-on-one sessions in the lobby of the Exchange Hotel, where he outlined his position in detail.

In 1860, Yancey left the national Democrats, who nominated Stephen A. Douglas, and supported John C. Breckenridge, nominated by the Southern Democrats. The Whigs nominated John Bell on the Constitutional Union ticket. And the Republicans nominated Abraham Lincoln, with a platform to prohibit slavery in the territories. Breckenridge carried most Alabama counties, but Lincoln won the election with the northern states. Talk of secession heightened.

Yancey was the leader of the "straight-out secessionists," opposed by "cooperationists" and Unionists adamantly against secession. As secession drew near, Winston County threatened to secede from Alabama to form the Free State of Winston. Popular vote for secession was 35,693 to 28,181 for the cooperationists.

Capital of the New Nation

From the day the Confederacy was announced in early February to the day its president, Jefferson Davis of Mississippi, would be sworn in on the steps of the capitol in Montgomery, Alabama's capital city grew from a population of 4,000 to 8,000. Many of these were men from throughout the Confederate states who wished to join in the new government and its cause.

On the Sunday night before Davis's inauguration, Yancey stepped onto the balcony outside the presidential suite in the Exchange Hotel in downtown Montgomery. He grasped the wide lapels of his black waistcoat and surveyed the crowd gathered around the Court Square fountain. His loud baritone voice carried the message of the Confederacy and in introducing Davis declared that "the man and the hour have met!"

On Monday morning, February 18, 1861, the first sounds of the day were the staccato thunder of cannons being discharged at daybreak by various military companies bivouacked around the city.

At 9 a.m., the Columbus Guards entered Court Square and marched their precision drill in front of the Exchange to collect the president-elect and accompany him to the capitol. Shortly after eleven the cannon sounded to announce the hour for the procession to form. As uniformed military fell into four lines, dressed in red and green and gray jackets with emblazoned epaulets, swords gleaming in the sunlight, and bayonets flashing, the officers called the groups into action.

Davis, a tall, dour, gaunt-faced man whose thick shock of dark hair kept falling onto his high forehead, walked slowly down the stairs of the Exchange. As he climbed aboard his carriage, he seemed preoccupied by the burdens that were about to descend upon his wide shoulders. Now and then as the six high-stepping gray horses pulled the carriage up the broad boulevard toward the capitol, he waved absently toward the cheering crowd. A military guard marched on each side of the carriage.

At 12:45 the carriage stopped amidst a throng that parted to let Davis climb to the top of the steps and stand between two great Corinthian columns. When the initial applause died down, Davis placed his left hand on the Bible while the President of the Confederate Congress, Howell Cobb of Georgia, swore him into office. He then delivered his inaugural address, outlining the mission of the new government, which he hoped would be carried out in peace.

That evening, he wrote his wife, who had remained at their home in Mississippi, "We are without machinery, without means, and threatened by a powerful opposition; but I do not despond, and will not shrink from the task imposed upon me."

Several weeks later, the first official flag of the Confederacy was presented to President Davis. Designed by Nicola Marschall of Marion at the request of Mrs. Napolean Lockett, it was made under the direction of the designer by several women at the Court Street Methodist Church in Montgomery. It had three red and white bars and its circle of seven white stars floated on a background of blue. The flag, known as the Stars and Bars, was carried to the capitol on the morning of March 4, where President Davis and Governor Andrew Berry Moore invited Letitia C. Tyler, granddaughter of U.S. President John Tyler, to raise it upon a flagpole lashed to the clock. Miss Tyler, who was visiting friends in Mount Meigs, a few miles east of Montgomery, hoisted the flag to the tune of *Dixie,* with the thundering blasts of cannons and the applause of hundreds gathered on the front lawn.

Davis's wife, Varina, arrived several weeks later, and they lived in the suite at the Exchange until a president's house could be obtained. The Congress and cabinet worked in an office building one block north of the Exchange on Commerce Street. The town's hotels were packed. Reporters from throughout the U.S. and abroad came to write about the new government and its leadership. Thomas Calhearne of *The Charleston Mercury* wrote that Montgomery was "a pig sty, if there ever was one. Very few self-respecting swine in this day and time live under the conditions of our Confederate capital after a downpour. When the streets of the downtown outside the hotel where I am lodged become soaked with rain, it is a shame the conditions of travel. Large puddles stand like lakes and backwaters of the Carolina Low Country. But Charleston and its environs have never seen the size of mosquitoes like the ones that swarm around the poor livestock that try to traverse these streets. Commerce Street on which I stay—only a short walk to the executive offices of the Confederacy, or a short wade through mud and debris, for the menace of the filth is beyond compare—is like a dump outside Poor Town or the stench outside privies of most town's slave sections." Sir William Howard Russell, the distinguished journalist from *The Times of London,* wrote, "I have rarely seen a more dull, lifeless place: it looks like a small Russian town in the interior." He described a meal at a plantation house where he dined with several cabinet members and their families. The squirrel stew was "near ineatable" and the baked possum "floated haplessly in the bowl of grease" and could be dipped from the thick hot fluid with chunks of cornbread.

The talk about war on the horizon was commonplace during the first weeks and months. Confederate Congressman Boykin Billingsley of Kentucky wrote his wife, "It is like the fear of what is about to happen is creeping in on us as we attempt to handle our everyday lives. I am a mere member of this august body, but I feel the hardships and the disciplines that rule the emotions of our leaders. I can see the wrinkles of deep despair cutting into the sallow cheeks of our president, Mr. Davis. I have never seen a man work so hard, so long, with so much problems weighing down upon his shoulders. I have heard people speak harshly about Mr. Lincoln, but I feel that he too is having a most difficult time, even though I do not understand his blasted stubbornness. As I walk the streets of this town I feel in every step that I am

The Confederate States Naval Foundry at Selma was burned by Union troops on April 5, 1865. The foundry was instrumental in providing ammunition to Southern soldiers as well as ironclad raiding ships used by the Confederate navy.

walking into a fire blazing so high—and so hot—that I will not be able to escape its torture."

On April 10, *The Montgomery Daily Mail* stated editorially, "All seem to concur that 'war is inevitable,' and they are 'ready, willing and awaiting' the firing of the first gun; and, with their muskets and knapsacks, are ready, at a moment's warning, to march in defense of their country's right and honor." On the next morning, President Davis telegraphed his commander, P. G. T. Beauregard, to demand evacuation of Fort Sumter off the coast of Charleston in South Carolina. That afternoon, under a flag of truce, Colonel James Chesnut Jr. and Captain Stephen D. Lee were rowed across the water from Charleston to deliver the ultimatum. Major Robert Anderson replied, "I will await the first shot. If you do not batter us to pieces we will be starved out in a few days." Beauregard relayed the message to Montgomery.

After several more attempts to seek surrender of the Fort, Davis, huddled with his advisors at the Exchange Hotel, sent word across the street to the telegraph office. From that office, still standing next to Court Square, where a brass plaque marks the event, the telegram was sent to Beauregard ordering the Confederates to open fire if Anderson did not surrender by 3:20 a.m.

On the night of April 12, more than 1,000 persons gathered outside the Exchange with a band to serenade their president. Although Davis was appreciative of the support, he sent word by Secretary of War Leroy Walker that he was too tired to speak. From the balcony, Walker told them "four of Sumter's big guns have been silenced." By late the next afternoon, Davis received word from General Beauregard that "we take possession of Fort Sumter tomorrow morning. No one killed on our side."

Within a few days, more volunteers flooded into Montgomery. More than a thousand slept in ditches, in alleys, streets, and announced that they were ready to fight the enemy.

On April 19, Davis sent Vice President Alexander Stephens to Richmond to secure Virginia's allegiance to the Confederacy. The next day, Colonel Robert E. Lee, who had been offered command of the Union forces, resigned from the U.S. Army.

Fighting the War

Within days, more battles broke out in South Carolina. The young men who passed through Montgomery were given a minimum of training, a sidearm or single-fire breech-loading rifles, some a uniform, and sent to fight hundreds of miles to the north and east. In late May, Jefferson Davis, his cabinet, and the Congress moved the government to Richmond to be close to the battlefront.

On the homefront, many women organized Ladies Aid Societies, making clothes from every scrap of wool or cotton they could find. In several towns, such as Selma, Montgomery, Anniston, and Mobile, ladies formed medical groups to take care of wounded soldiers when they were returned. Women took no part in the election process that formed the political basis for secession, but few spoke out in opposition. Women worked in textile plants and in arms industries such as the Selma Arsenal.

In April of 1862, federal troops captured Huntsville, where fifteen locomotives, the telegraph office and equipment, and two hundred prisoners were taken. Refugees fled to the South.

In late April, the word of Shiloh spread southward. Across Alabama, General Nathan Bedford Forrest became a household name and an instant hero. Tales were told of his being warned of Union troops in Tuscumbia, riding with his men into battle, and saving the Confederates, who were outnumbered more than two-to-one.

After Shiloh, several thousand captured Union troops were brought into Alabama. Some were imprisoned in Tuscaloosa, others in Montgomery and Cahaba. Of the 650 prisoners of war sheltered in an old cotton warehouse in Montgomery, some 198 died by December 14, 1862, when the facility was closed and the prisoners moved.

There were several Union raids into Alabama during the war. On one from Chickasaw to Tuscumbia, across to Blountsville and Gadsden, General Forrest earned the nickname "wizard of the saddle" when his cavalry troops forded a river and cut off the Yankees before they got into Georgia. A young Alabama girl, Emma Sansom, became a heroine after word spread of her showing Forrest the place where he could cross Black Creek and stop the Union forces.

Admiral Raphael Semmes had been a lawyer in Mobile before he was commissioned a commander in the Confederate Navy. In 1861, the CSS *Sumter* under Semmes's command captured eighteen Northern ships before being blockaded. Semmes's next ship was the CSS *Alabama*, a much faster and sleeker design. With this command, Semmes became a Confederate hero.

A hero from Mobile was Raphael Semmes, who commanded the CSS *Alabama* after it was constructed in Liverpool, England, and was anchored off the shore of Wales. During the next two years it attacked Union merchant ships all over the world, capturing a total of sixty-nine vessels and cargo worth at least $5.1 million.

After the *Alabama* sank the USS *Hatteras* off the coast of Galveston in 1863, it was challenged in the water off France by the USS *Kearsarge*, which was much larger, had stronger guns and fresh powder, and was partially ironclad. Within two hours of battle, the *Alabama* went down. Semmes was rescued by an English yachtsman.

When Admiral David G. Farragut sailed into Mobile Bay in 1864, he was prepared to sink every Confederate ship in sight. The U.S. iron-clad *Tecumseh* opened fire. Guns from Fort Morgan on the east blasted across the water. The *Tecumseh* also caught fire from Fort Gaines on Dauphin Island. It sank. Torpedoes were fired on the USS *Brooklyn*, stalling the attack. That was when Farragut issued his famous command, "Damn the torpedoes! Full speed ahead!" After the *Tennessee* was hit by cannon blast and was rammed by an ironclad, it raised the white flag, ending the battle of Mobile Bay.

During the last days of the War, General James Wilson led his raiders south to Jasper, Elyton, Tannehill, Tuscaloosa, Montevallo, Brierfield, and Selma. He fought and burned and destroyed the armament factories, the ironworks, the arsenals, and the school for cadets.

On the morning of April 11, 1865, General Abraham Buford, commanding the Confederate forces in Montgomery, ordered his men to haul all cotton bales from warehouses near the waterfront. With them, he barricaded all the roads leading into the state capital. The remaining 85,000 bales were stacked in an open field and burned. An evacuation plan was devised if defense failed. That evening, however, Buford received word "to attempt no defense in Montgomery." He was ordered to march east immediately to Columbus, Georgia.

Governor Thomas Watts and his cabinet followed the troops southeast.

At 3 a.m. on April 12, Montgomery Mayor W. L. Coleman and nine prominent citizens rode southwest to a spot near Catoma Creek. Holding a flag of truce, they were met by General Wilson and accompanied him and his troops into town.

Wilson hoisted the U.S. flag atop the capitol and gave orders that no one was to be harmed and no property was to be destroyed. He ordered his troops to comb the town to find anyone they might help in case of an emergency.

Montgomery was put under the command of General Edward McCook, who promised "full protection" and warned his troops once again against attacks on property or persons. He made his headquarters in the Exchange Hotel.

Four days earlier, Lee had surrendered to General U.S. Grant at Appomattox Courthouse in Virginia. The word did not reach Montgomery for several more days.

Not only did the end of the war free slaves, it changed an entire region's economic system forever. Alabama sustained fewer structural losses than other states such as Georgia, South Carolina, and Virginia. However, wartime industry was destroyed by Wilson's raiders. Four buildings at the University of Alabama were burned. Several hundred miles of rails were lost by the railroad companies. Montgomery lost three steamboats, a foundry, and a rolling mill.

Faced with Reconstruction, Alabamians attempted to circumvent the rule of their captors. However, military occupation brought with it the Freedman's Bureau, with its ideas of equal justice, labor, education, relief, medical aid, and political education. In some instances, the new black citizens were allowed to purchase public lands. However, the constitutional convention of 1865 did not make blacks equal under the law. It asked the legislature to pass laws to protect blacks. When the legislature met the following year, the laws it enacted became known as the Alabama Black Code, regulating what work the race could do, how much workers would be paid, and how blacks would conduct themselves in society.

Reconstruction

After President Lincoln was assassinated, President Andrew Johnson attempted to carry out Lincoln's plan for reconstruction. However, in 1866, over the president's veto, Congress passed the Civil Rights Act outlining Radical Republican Reconstruction. This plan punished the defeated Southern states. For the first time, black voters outnumbered whites. Of one hundred delegates to a new constitutional convention, ninety-six were Republican, including eighteen blacks. Laws changed radically.

In many communities across the state, Ku Klux Klan organizations were founded, patterning themselves after a group that first met in Pulaski, Tennessee, in 1865, and soon came under the leadership of Nathan Bedford Forrest. In essence, the KKK was formed to intimidate blacks from exercising their new privileges of citizenship.

Railroads began rebuilding across the state. By 1870, Governor William E. Smith worked out a way whereby the state's railway system received some $4 million in bonds to build 250 miles of track for the Alabama and Chattanooga County.

During this time, Bourbon Democrats began making strides to move into power. More Jim Crow laws were enacted. A monetary system began to grow. The average size of farms dropped from more than three hundred acres to little more than fifty acres. Although cotton remained the leading cash crop, its production was drastically changed. The new farmers came up with the sharecropper system, which remained in place for almost a century. Toward the turn of the century, an infrastructure of agriculture, manufacturing, and industry would emerge, pointing toward a time of greater growth in the twentieth century.

In 1871, after railway lines of the South and North and the Alabama and Chattanooga crossed in a valley in the north-central section, Birmingham was founded. A Montgomery banker, Josiah Morris, spent $100,000 to buy 4,150 acres in the valley. He formed the Elyton Land Company, which began laying out streets, and prepared to auction lots. The first, at the intersection of First Avenue North and 19th Street,

Sloss Furnace in Birmingham, where coal from the hills around the town was used to heat the ore that was also dug from the earth to make quality pig iron used in the production of steel. In the late 1800s and the first half of the twentieth century, mining of coal and ore became a major industry in Alabama's largest city.

sold for $100. The city that had incorporated with 1,200 residents in 1871 grew to more than 4,000 in two years. A cholera epidemic that year killed 128, and several thousand fled back to the farms from which they had come, but a sturdy 1,200 were remaining in 1875 to fight the problems of frontier life. The town's future was set some ten years later, when three industrialists, Henry deBardeleben, Colonel J. W. Sloss, and Truman Aldrich, opened two blast furnaces to produce pig iron, using local products. On Thanksgiving Day of 1899, the first steel was produced by Tennessee Coal & Iron Company, 91 percent of which was owned by New Yorkers and three percent by Alabamians. New capital and management were infused into the company when U.S. Steel bought TCI in 1907.

Into the Twentieth Century

The constitutional convention of 1901 produced a document that is still in effect in Alabama. It repealed much of the Reconstruction laws but was written in a language of racist bitterness exceeding all others. In a statewide vote, it was ratified 108,613 in favor to 81,734 opposed.

While Orville and Wilbur Wright opened their first school for pilots near Montgomery in the first decade of the new century, women began organizing around the state to fight for suffrage. While they were gathered, most also sought to abolish liquor sales in the state. Julia Tutwiler headed the Women's Christian Temperance Union, which also spoke out for prison and child-labor reform. Miss Tutwiler was an author and an outspoken leader. She wrote "Alabama," which became the state song.

Another outstanding female who came of age in the early years of the new century was Helen Keller, who was born in Tuscumbia. When she was eighteen months old she became blind and deaf. With help of teacher Annie Sullivan, who came to the Keller home of Ivy Green to teach her when Helen was seven, she learned the alphabet. She graduated from Radcliffe with honors, worked with other hearing- and sight-impaired people, wrote many books and articles, and developed into an excellent and powerful speaker. As such, she became a symbol of courage and an inspiration to countless many.

Alabama's contribution to literature has been varied, but has consistently reflected the character and history of the state. One of the earlier and more popular books was Raphael Semmes's *Memoirs of Service Afloat, during the War Between the States*, published in 1869.

Sutton S. Scott was born in Huntsville, practiced law, and served with the Confederacy as commissioner of Indian affairs. His *Southbooke* was a collection of novelette, poetry, and some prose pieces. His *Mobilians*, published in 1898, glorified the South and its way of life.

Augusta Evans Wilson was born in Columbus, Georgia, lived for a while in Texas, and settled in Mobile in 1849. There she wrote her wartime novel, *Macaria; or, Altars of Sacrifice*, strong Southern propaganda. Best known for *St. Elmo's*, which became a bestseller in 1866, she went on to write four other novels.

Francis Bartow Lloyd was city editor of *The Montgomery Advertiser* when he began writing his Rufus Sanders sketches, a column with an enormous following about a character on the frontier who was a whimsical con man. A collection was published in 1898 under the title *Sketches of Country Life: Humor, Wisdom, and Pathos from the 'Sage of Rocky Creek'.*

William C. Handy, who became known as the Father of the Blues, was born in Florence. His father was a preacher and was said to have influenced his son's writing of such bawdy ballads as "St. Louis Blues" and "Memphis Blues." Most of his work was done after he moved to Memphis.

Howard Weeden became famous as a painter of portraits of Alabama slaves. His paintings were exhibited in Europe in the 1890s. London-born Roderick McKenzie arrived in Mobile in 1872. He painted a historical mural in the dome of the capitol in Montgomery. Anne Goldthwaite of Montgomery traveled widely but was known primarily for her landscapes of the Black Belt. Kelly Fitzpatrick studied in Paris and started the Dixie Art Colony at Wetumpka. He also helped found the Alabama Art League and the Montgomery Museum of Fine Arts.

Downtown Mobile, with its statue of Confederate hero Admiral Raphael Semmes, has a French-style atmosphere rivaled only by New Orleans. Mobile is the home of the oldest Mardi Gras in the United States.

When the Great War started, it seemed doubtful that Alabama would play a large part. However, 74,000 Alabamians were inducted into the army; more were sent from the Alabama National Guard's Forty-second "Rainbow" Division. The Guard had first been called to duty in 1916 to join General John Pershing in putting down the revolt in Mexico, led by Pancho Villa. When they came home, the camp at Vandiver Park, about six miles northeast of Montgomery, was renamed Camp Sheridan, which would become the home of the Thirty-seventh Division from Ohio, there for training before being shipped to the battlefront in France.

The Jazz Age

One young lieutenant stationed at Sheridan was F. Scott Fitzgerald, whose first novel had just been turned down by Scribners. During the summer of 1918, he met a local belle, Zelda Sayre, who had recently graduated from Sidney Lanier High School and had already made a name for herself as the most beautiful dancer in the region. They courted for two years, until they were married in New York on April 20, 1920, in the chapel at St. Patrick's Cathedral. By that time, he had rewritten the novel and called it *This Side of Paradise*, and it became a bestseller. Fitzgerald went on to give the decade of the 1920s its name, The Jazz Age, and his lovely young wife was the personification of The Flapper.

Tallulah Bankhead, a native of Huntsville whose father, John, was majority leader of the U.S. Senate and whose uncle William was Speaker of the House, spent much of her time growing up in Montgomery, where her aunt, Marie Bankhead Owens, was director of the state archives. Miss Bankhead became one of the most successful actresses on the Broadway stage and in movies.

The 1920s were complex and generally prosperous years for Alabama. A populist politician named Bibb Graves, born in Hope Hull, south of Montgomery, a graduate of the civil engineering school at the University of Texas and law school at Yale, served two terms as legislator and lost his first bid for governor in 1922. Four years later, he had more backers: a coalition of Evangelical Protestants who liked his views on prohibition, the Ku Klux Klan (because he was a member), organized labor, veterans of World War I, and educators. Big industry from Birmingham and Black Belt planters backed Lieutenant Governor Charles S. McDowell Jr. of Eufaula.

Soon after he took the oath of office in 1927, Graves removed convict labor from mines. Instead, he put them to work on road construction crews, in plants making clothes, car tags, and road signs. He aggressively sought new industry and brought it to the state. His tax reform package produced additional revenue for state services. With money from taxes on tobacco, he set about building schools throughout rural Alabama.

Motorized vehicles increased from 16,000 in 1920 to 70,000 in 1930. The Alabama Farm Bureau Federation, begun in 1919 as a non-partisan, non-political business organization for farmers, prospered under the leadership of Edward A. O'Neal III of Florence. By 1926 it had 26,000 members and had departed from its original stated intent. Throughout the rest of the century it became one of the most powerful political forces and lobbying organizations in the state.

Expanding Horizons

During the decade, Octavus Roy Cohen of Birmingham wrote numerous magazine stories and led a literary group, "the Loafers," which included Edgar Valentine Smith, who had three O. Henry prize stories, and James Saxon Childers, who was a Rhodes Scholar and wrote novels while teaching at Birmingham-Southern College. Marie Bankhead Owen was the state archivist and wrote eight volumes of Alabama history, three novels, and several plays. T. S. Stribling won the Pulitzer Prize for *The Store*, about life in the Tennessee River Valley. It was part of a trilogy of novels about north Alabama. William March of Mobile wrote *Company K*, which was one of the outstanding novels about World War I, and *The Bad Seed*, a bestseller and later a successful motion picture. Sara Haardt of Montgomery wrote numerous literary short stories and married the famed Baltimore editor H. L. Mencken. Zelda Sayre Fitzgerald returned with her husband to Montgomery for a short period in 1931 and '32, when she wrote her only novel, *Save Me The Waltz*.

Tallulah Bankhead was born in Huntsville but lived in Montgomery as a teenager with her aunt, Marie Bankhead Owen. She became one of the best-known and highly praised actresses of her time. She was known for her salty language, her outrageous antics, and her superb beauty.

The Great Depression

When the Great Depression struck in the 1930s, Scott Fitzgerald said one of the reasons he liked Montgomery so much was "they don't talk of the Depression." But it was felt in the businesses and the political halls. Middle-class families slid into the poor category. None but the very rich had what they had had previously. In Birmingham it was said, "When the steel industry coughed, Birmingham caught pneumonia." And when U.S. Steel closed its furnaces, Birmingham was at a standstill, affecting everybody in the community.

Although the economy was bleak, Alabamians helped themselves.

Downtown Birmingham in the 1930s was a thriving metropolis. It grew up so fast it was nicknamed "the Magic City," because it appeared like magic. In 1873 it had 1,200 residents. When a cholera epidemic hit that summer, 128 died. The economic panic of the following year almost bankrupted the Elyton Land Company, the corporation that founded the city.

Few farmers went without food. A native of Alabama, Thad Holt, presided over the state's relief program. Later he became head of the Works Progress Administration, and Aubrey Williams, a poor boy when he grew up in Birmingham, became a part of President Franklin Delano Roosevelt's New Deal. The Civilian Conservation Corps enrolled about 67,000 young Alabamians from 1933 to 1942. These young men not only learned skills, they put the skills to practical use. The state parks system that was started by the legislature in 1923 as part of the Alabama Forestry Commission was expanded by the CCC. Seventeen state parks were constructed with rustic cabins, hiking trails, dams, lakes, and picnic facilities. Many of these youngsters became the nucleus of the army from Alabama when World War II broke out in the early 1940s.

New Hotels

In the last quarter of the nineteenth century and the beginnings of the twentieth, tourism once again became a factor in the Alabama economy. The Woodstock Iron Company, which built Anniston as a model city, constructed the Anniston Inn in 1884 at the cost of $260,000. The dining room alone cost $27,000. Built in the graceful Queen Anne tradition, it had wide verandahs across all the entire first three floors. Located on twenty acres of beautifully landscaped grounds with a lake in the middle, the interior was floored throughout in southern pine, with large sitting rooms, dining rooms, and parlors on the first floor and a wide grand staircase of polished oak. After being elected vice-president of the U.S. in 1893, Adlai Stevenson was entertained at the Inn by Dr. T. W. Ayers. When General John J. Pershing visited Camp McClellan in 1919, he was entertained at the Inn with a possum dinner. Colonel Harry N. Ayers, commander of the local American Legion lodge, served as host. In 1923 the building burned, and it was never rebuilt.

Throughout the second half of the nineteenth century the Battle House was Mobile's finest after it replaced the Mansion House that burned. On his way to be inaugurated president of the Confederacy, Jefferson Davis stayed in one of the 240 rooms. Among the Confederate generals who stayed at the Battle House were Braxton Bragg, P. G.

T. Beauregard and E. R. B. Canby. After the Civil War, Ulysses S. Grant overnighted before he was elected president. And Millard Fillmore stayed after his presidency.

In 1889, the Gadsden Land and Improvement Company opened the Bellevue Hotel with a hundred rooms. From the fourth floor observation tower one had unobstructed views of the mountains and the lush valley around Gadsden. The hotel burned to the ground in 1912 and was never rebuilt. Foundation was laid for a new eight-story hotel, but building funds ran out before it could be completed.

One of the finest hotels in the state was Borden-Wheeler Springs at Fruithurst in Cleburne County, where a colony of Swedish settlers planted vineyards in the last years of the nineteenth century. The turn-of-the-century hotel had a hundred rooms, with wide porticoes overlooking the mountains covered with pine, maple, oak, elm, sweet, and black gum trees. Cottages with electric lights, running water, and maid service were built around the manicured grounds. The water at the springs was said to be "a close second to Ponce de Leon's famed 'Fountain of Youth.'" In the early twentieth century the Seaboard Railroad provided excursion rates to the resort. One-way fare from Birmingham was $2.77 and a season ticket $4.60. Rates to and from Atlanta were slightly lower. Rates at the hotel were $15 a week, $50 a month. In 1935, fire swept the hotel and twenty cottages; it was never rebuilt.

In 1884 an inn was built at Mentone by Dr. Frank Caldwell of Pennsylvania. The two-story frame structure with fifty-seven rooms became known as the Mentone Springs Hotel. The wide porches overlooked the mountains and the valley. Water was provided from deep wells. The hotel has changed ownership a number of times through the years. Most recently it has been operated as a bed-and-breakfast.

The Morris Hotel opened in 1894 in downtown Birmingham. Its dining room was a showplace. Fine cuisine was served. When Josiah Morris first built it, the building held offices, but it was turned into a hotel four years later. In 1958 the building was razed. It had been the last standing vestige to the memory of one of Birmingham's founding fathers.

Civil Rights and Wrongs

In the latter half of the twentieth century, life changed in Alabama. In December of 1955, a black seamstress named Rosa Parks refused to give up her seat on a city bus in Montgomery. She was arrested for violating the city's segregation ordinance, a law she and the National Association for the Advancement of Colored People challenged all the way to the U.S. Supreme Court. As a result of her arrest, the Montgomery Improvement Association was formed and a young minister named Martin Luther King Jr. became president. Through the leadership of a pullman car porter, E. D. Nixon, who had worked with

Rosa Parks, the seamstress whose refusal to give up her seat on a Montgomery city bus was a protest heard around the world, walks between two Montgomery ministers, R. B. Binnion and H. J. Palmer. When she was arrested for challenging the law forbidding black people from sitting in the front rows of the public transportation, the leadership of the Montgomery Improvement Association called for a boycott of the buses. That successful boycott and Mrs. Parks's subsequent victory in the U.S. Supreme Court became the cornerstone of the Civil Rights Movement.

Dr. Martin Luther King Jr. steps from a city bus in Montgomery at the end of the year-long bus boycott.

A. Philip Randolph when he organized the porter's union, King and the MIA led a year-long boycott of the buses which was in essence the beginning of the Civil Rights Movement. In November of 1956, the high court upheld a finding that overturned the city's segregation ordinance. When the court order became final, King and other boycott leaders boarded a bus and sat in the front section, giving a symbolic end to the boycott.

In the early 1960s, Eugene "Bull" Connor reigned as Birmingham's police commissioner. Calling for the disbursement of demonstrations in Kelly Ingram Park with his bullhorn, Connor brought in firemen with hoses and police with dogs. He turned both loose on the crowd that was gathered across the street from the Sixteenth Street Baptist Church.

In June of 1963, Governor George Wallace, who had campaigned vigorously on the promise that he would not allow desegregation of schools in Alabama, stood in the schoolhouse door at the University of Alabama in a well-orchestrated symbolic protest. Wallace then moved aside in order that black students Vivian Malone and James Hood could register while being accompanied by federal marshals.

On Sunday, September 16, 1963, a bomb exploded under the steps

The first inauguration of Governor George C. Wallace was watched closely by the nation. With his son, George Jr., his wife, Lurleen, and two daughters, Bobbie Jo and Peggy Sue, Wallace smiles for the camera before tossing down the gauntlet and declaring, "Segregation today! Segregation tomorrow! Segregation forever!" Wallace's wife Lurleen ran for governor next and won. She died in office. He won the office three more times, twice in the 1970s and once in 1980s. He was paralyzed by an assassin's bullet while running for president in 1972.

of the Sixteenth Street Baptist Church in Birmingham, killing four young girls who were attending Sunday school.

In Selma in 1965, local black activists were joined by national civil rights leaders such as John Lewis, a member of the Student Non-Violent Coordinating Committee, in demonstrations to protest the unfair treatment of blacks trying to register to vote. The demonstrators attempted to march from Selma to Montgomery, but state troopers and sheriff's deputies, some mounted on horseback wielding billyclubs, others with dogs and tear gas, attacked as the procession crossed over the Edmund Pettus Bridge. Television news cameras recorded the brutal assault. That evening, the entire nation was stunned as it watched the turmoil on the national news broadcasts.

King went to federal court in Montgomery asking that his marchers be allowed to demonstrate peacefully on the U.S. highway. District Judge Frank M. Johnson Jr., who already had Alabama's schools under his jurisdiction, ruled that under the U.S. Constitution, the marchers had the right. On March 21, 1965, the march resumed from the Brown Chapel AME Church where King stated, "Walk together, children, don't you get weary, and it will lead us to the promised land. And Alabama will be the new Alabama, and America will be the new America!" Four days later King led 25,000 followers through the streets of Montgomery to the capitol. He told the crowd that "they told us we wouldn't get here," but, he added, "we ain't gonna let nobody turn us around."

By 1969, there were more than 295,000 blacks registered to vote in Alabama, and that number has more than doubled since then. Black officeholders were elected to office. A black justice was elected statewide to the Supreme Court. Black legislators sat in both chambers of the legislature. Black political leaders held enormous clout with all elected officials.

The State Changes

Alabama changed in many other ways. From Birmingham's steel industry that controlled much of the state's economy with its Sloss Furnace that wheezed and coughed and spat out fiery yellow products and by-products, to the stevedores of the docks in Mobile, to King Cotton through the Tennessee River Valley, the state changed to a modern society. With the beginning of the Marshall Space Flight Center and Redstone Arsenal to the ultra-modern industry that grew up from garages to gigantic glass-and-steel facilities, Huntsville boomed from a country town to a developed city. Birmingham leaped from being an industrial monstrosity to a medical research and technological center. By the 1980s, Birmingham's leading employer was the medical industry that grew up with the University of Alabama's Medical Center. Insurance companies developed throughout the twentieth century, led by Liberty National. Following World War II, Winton M. "Red" Blount made a name for himself by building the family business, Blount Brothers Construction, into an international corporation with projects from Arabia to Alaska. In the late 1960s he became president of the U.S. Chamber of Commerce, and President Richard Nixon appointed him Postmaster General of the U.S. Blount engineered the new post office, bringing the bureaucracy into the mainstream of business and making it pay its way. Back at the helm of Blount Brothers, he expanded its horizons to include construction of the Superdome in New Orleans and the University of Riyad in Saudi Arabia.

Tourism Grows

Once again in the 1980s and '90s, Alabama's tourism industry made great leaps forward to become the second largest money-maker in the state. By 1995, tourism was a $4.5 billion-a-year business. From the Space and Rocket Center at Huntsville, where hundreds of children went to Space Camp every year, to the USS *Alabama*, permanently docked in Mobile Bay, millions of tourists annually came to Alabama to seek pleasure. From weekend football games at the universities of Alabama and Auburn to Olympic soccer matches in Birmingham in the summer of 1996, more tourist dollars than ever before promised to fill the local coffers with green-back dollars.

Entertainers

Alabama entertainers made big names for themselves throughout the twentieth century.

Hank Williams was a tall, skinny country boy from Butler County who played on Montgomery radio before he caught the attention of producers of the Grand Ole Opry in Nashville and the Dixie Jamboree in Shreveport. His songs, from "Your Cheatin' Heart" to "I'm So Lonesome I Could Cry," continue to be perennial hits on the country and popular charts. People from all over the globe visit Hank Williams's grave atop a hillside in Montgomery's Oakwood Cemetery.

Nat King Cole was born in Montgomery. When he came home to sing in Birmingham in the sixties, racists in the audience pelted him with eggs and attacked him on stage. Today his birthplace is sought as a tourist attraction.

Lionel Richie was raised in Tuskegee, where he formed the Commodores and began making top hits for Motown Records. Many of his tunes, such as "Three Times a Lady" and "Endless Love," have topped the pop charts. Randy Owens and cousin Teddy Wayne Gentry were raised on the mountain near Fort Payne, where they started the group Alabama, and in 1979 put their music and the state on the map with a number-one hit, "My Home's in Alabama." In the early eighties the group was named Entertainer of the Year five years in a row.

In literature, Alabama also prevailed, with a Monroeville native, Nelle Harper Lee, winning the Pulitzer Prize with her poignant novel *To Kill a Mockingbird*, which was made into an Academy Award-winning motion picture. A play from the book is produced every year in Monroeville by local citizens. Walker Percy, a native of Birmingham, became a literary giant with such books as *The Moviegoer* and *Love in the Ruins* and numerous essays. Babs H. Deal brought her hometown of Scottsboro to life as the fictitious Bellefonte in novels such as *Acres of Afternoon,* and *Three O'Clock in the Morning,* and *High Lonesome World.* Paul Hemphill, a native of Birmingham, was praised widely for his novels, *Long Gone* and *King of the Road,* as well as high-styled non-fiction, *Leaving Birmingham* and *The Nashville Sound.* Birmingham novelist Vickie Covington has received national notice for her work in *Bird of Paradise* and *The Last Hotel for Women,* the latter of which characterizes Bill Connor in the pages of the narrative and portrays the mean streets of downtown Birmingham when Connor was police commissioner. Dennis Covington's *Salvation on Sand Mountain* has received honors for

Hank Williams was the most famous country songwriter and singer of his generation. Born near Georgiana, he grew up in Montgomery, where he won a talent contest at the Empire Theater when he was a teenager. He later joined the Grand Ole Opry and the Dixie Jamboree, where he sang his own songs, including "Your Cheatin' Heart," "Cold, Cold Heart," "Kowliga," and "I'm So Lonesome I Could Cry."

39

The Alabama capitol was moved to Montgomery by the Legislature in 1847. The new State Capitol building was the home of just one legislative session before it burned to the ground in 1849. It was rebuilt the next year. Wings were added in the early 1900s. In the early 1980s it underwent major restoration and today houses the governor's office and offices of other constitutional officeholders. The legislative chambers are furnished as they were in the mid-nineteenth century.

its word picture of life in northeast Alabama among snake-handling fundamentalists. Winston Groom of Mobile authored several fine novels, including *Gone the Sun* about a native son who returns to rework the local newspaper, before his short novel, *Forest Gump,* became a runaway hit as a movie.

Birmingham native Howell Raines won a Pulitzer Prize for journalism for his moving account of growing up in Ensley with the black maid who taught him much about the human condition. His novel, *Whiskey Man,* and his oral history of the Civil Rights Movement, *My Soul is Rested,* have been singled out as splendid literary accomplishments.

A number of excellent motion pictures have been made in and about Alabama, including Birmingham novelist Charles Gaines's *Stay Hungry* with Sally Field and Arnold Schwarzenegger, Montgomery screenwriter John Cork's tender story of a black maid and the white family she works for in *A Long Walk Home,* and *Blue Sky,* which was made in Selma with Tommy Lee Jones and Jessica Lange. The television film about the old Negro baseball league, *Soul of the Game,* was partially shot at the restored Rickwood Field, the home of the Birmingham Barons.

Winton Blount and his wife, Carolyn, gave beautiful rolling hills in east Montgomery and more than $20 million to build the Carolyn Blount Theatre, home of the Alabama Shakespeare Festival, arguably the finest dramatic facility in the world. Thousands of school children from around the state enjoy bus rides to the theatre, where they experience first-class drama and learn from the best in the business. And tens of thousands of visitors come to Alabama to see the plays—not only Shakespeare's but modern drama, musicals, and comedies—in the two theaters under one roof. After the Southern Writers Project was founded to develop plays by minority and Southern playwrights, *Lizard* by Dennis Covington became a hit and was chosen as part of the Cultural Olympiad in Atlanta in 1996, and Anniston's Randy Hall wrote *Grover* about the inimitable Pulitzer Prize-winning editor of *The Montgomery Advertiser* who fought the Ku Klux Klan in the 1920s and 30s.

A New Beginning

In 1994, Fob James, a native of Lanett who had been elected governor as a Democrat in 1978, did what no other Alabama politician had ever accomplished when he switched parties and ran as a Republican and won, becoming the first to serve as governor from both political parties. Steadfast in his conviction that prayer in school should be legal, he promised to fight the same battle he had started in his first term. Positioning himself as a pro-business politician, he began aggressively to seek out-of-state industry, although he was the first to say he would not "give away the state" to lure relocation to Alabama.

On the threshold of the twenty-first century, Alabama opened its arms and beckoned to the outside world to become part of its quality of life: where small towns still exist, where beaches at Gulf Shores are open to family vacations, where industry is clean and where growth is seen as a virtue.

NORTH ALABAMA

Multi-colored beauty fills the skies above north Alabama during Decatur's annual balloon-flying event.

This is the river, a Chickamauga wild and irreconcilable, cutting grandly and senselessly through a mountain range to seek a new valley, a southward river that swings north again to join a blue water it should never have known. And this is the land that belongs to the river, this earth between narrows and bend out of all the earth that verges on the river's banks in its long traveling which is peculiarly its own because it too is wild and irreconcilable, not easy to be settled and tamed yet with warm pockets of growth and comfort and home among its wildness. This is the land of violence and differentness, a land that has never known peace. It is wild and craggy, back-boned by the heavy, massive sweep of south-tapering mountains, wombed by creeks and coves cutting away from the deep river.

Dunbars's Cove
by Borden Deal

44

Right, original instruments on display at the W. C. Handy Birthplace Museum and Library in Florence.

Opposite, performers at Florence's annual week-long W. C. Handy Music Festival.

Overleaf, Lower Factory Falls in Marion County.

The banks of the winding Tennessee River in northwest Alabama encompassed the whole world for me from the time I can remember what music sounded like until I grew into my rambling shoes. My hometown, Sheffield, is the heart of Muscle Shoals, a cluster of small towns named for two prominent local features: the freshwater mussels we spell "muscle," and the great and treacherous rocky shoals scattered about the bustling waterway. Sheffield sits on the south bank of the river. A mile-long bridge connects us with the town of Florence, where high atop a scenic bluff sits the birthplace of W. C. Handy, the "Father of the Blues."

A Call to Assembly
by Willie Ruff

50

It wasn't always thus. The Birmingham area in the 1990s stands in sharp contrast to the Birmingham of earlier decades—a smoky, dangerous though often profitable place, a town out of step with Alabama's rural heritage, a city that would become the state's economic powerhouse and one of the South's most important metropolises. As the largest city in Alabama, Birmingham, the nation's 46th largest Metropolitan Statistical Area with a population of 907,810, has more than twenty percent of the state's population, households, and businesses. About thirty-two percent of all state payroll dollars are dispersed in the metro area.

Birmingham grew from the ground up, literally. The ground. The earth and the minerals that lay within the folds of soil and rock; those were the genesis of the Magic City.

Birmingham: Magic City Renaissance
by Joe O'Donnell

The Birmingham skyline at night.

The West Fork of Little River,
just above DeSoto Falls.

Left, the view from Rock Garden, below the summit of Mt. Cheaha, Cheaha State Park.

Overleaf, fly fishing at Oak Mountain State Park

Pages 62–63, the *Delta Queen* on the Tennessee River, east of Guntersville Locks.

This rugged northern reach had been occupied originally by an outlaw amalgam of Chickasaw, Cherokee, and Creek Indians, rogues, and descendants of rogues from the nearby tribal areas, who had enjoyed fighting among themselves almost as much as they had enjoyed fighting the stiff-necked, righteous, independent whites who came to oust them. They had fallen back deeper into the coves as the Bible-toting men with towheaded children and timeworn wives had pressed them harder and harder, until at the end the army had been called in to clear them out and ship them to Oklahoma. Operation Cattle Drive had not been a success; there were too many hidden coves, too many razorback ridges for an Indian to disappear over . . .

The Loser
by Borden Deal

59

To do a job right, a person needs the right tools. Above, Harrison Brothers Hardware in Huntsville is the oldest store of its kind in the state. To the right, a worker at the 1819 John Boardman Print Shop at Huntsville's Constitution Village prepares an early printing press to turn out a one-page handout like so many of the state's earliest newspapers. The type was handset and rolled down to actually press the type onto the paper to make an imprint. In the foreground is the state constitution.

Left, DeSoto Falls, DeSoto State Park.

Overleaf, Village Creek in Jefferson County.

We walked down the path to the well-house, attracted by the fragrance of the honeysuckle with which it was covered. Someone was drawing water and my teacher placed my hand under the spout. As the cool stream gushed over one hand she spelled into the other the word water, first slowly, then rapidly. I stood still, my whole attention fixed upon the motions of her fingers. Suddenly I felt a misty consciousness as of something forgotten—a thrill of returning thought; and somehow the mystery of language was revealed to me. I knew then that 'w-a-t-e-r' meant the wonderful cool something that was flowing over my hand. That living word awakened my soul, gave it light, hope, joy, set it free.

The Story of my Life
by Helen Keller

Right, gaslights show the way to the entrance of Birmingham's Civil Rights Institute, which houses a pathway through the experience of the years since the days when demonstrators were abused and the Sixteenth Street Baptist Church was blown up. Today the area is a tourist attraction including the church, the Institute, and Kelly Ingram Park.

Overleaf, *Praying Ministers* in Kelly Ingram Park honors clergy who assisted demonstrators during the Civil Rights Movement.

70

Sports are great attractions for many. Whether attending a NASCAR auto race at Talladega as thousands do every year or playing a round of golf on one of the state's many pristine golf courses, the sports enthusiast will be satisfied with Alabama's cornucopia of thrills.

Left, Cheaha Creek in Talladega National Forrest.

Overleaf, Alabama Music Hall of Fame in Tuscumbia.

As people have retreated from Clay County, the wood-lands have advanced, retaking land once laboriously cleared for crops, and giving the hillsides something of the feel of frontier wilderness, with relics, and maybe ghosts, from Indian wanderings and battles, with the abandoned shafts left from gold, graphite, and mica mines, with coons, and white-tailed fawns, and possums with their young, who die by scores along the road, but in the woods take work to catch.

Although the land is no longer all your sustenance, and even if it fails, you still can eat, it surrounds you always, fading at winter into bare-branched hardwood and brown, close-eaten pastures that stretch tight over every hilly undulation, then breaking green again in spring, with the spangled lace of dogwoods, and the sound of hungry bees. You venture out for the logs that fuel wood-fired heaters, for game, or to walk and be alone. Clear land is often sowed in pasture grass, and filled with cows of all descriptions, some for profit, some as a hobby that offers the excuse to ride a tractor, to make hay and tramp around, a farmer on your own piece of ground. Garden patches, and even tethered mules, lie within a block or two of Ashland's city square, and many women can and dry the way their mothers did, as much from habit as necessity.

You Always Think of Home
by Pamela Grundy

Right, Borden Creek in the Sipsey Wilderness Area of Bankhead National Forest.

Overleaf, Blount County's Horton Mill Covered Bridge, which stands 70 feet above the Calvert Prong of the Warrior River.

M ost roads defy an unsettled country, bringing as they do the order of law and civilized habits. But this sandy trail left no such impression. It seemed to be on sufferance of the high-towering forest and steep low mountains which at any moment threatened to press together the trees and re-take it. And I had the absurd feeling that it was only waiting for my entrance to close behind and trap me. As the reassuring sun lifted, I threw off the weight, as I then thought, of these morbid thoughts and started out, southeast by east. After an hour I began to climb the slopes of the miniature mountain. What fears I had left vanished in the exertions of the climb. A good sweat will do wonders for a man.

The Long Night
by Andrew Lytle

Shuttle Park at the U.S. Space and Rocket Center in Huntsville.

In the 1970s, engineers in Huntsville moved on to a new stage in the exploration of space. They began to work on the space shuttle, a huge machine that blasted off like a rocket and flew into space but then returned to earth and landed like an airplane. After firing, the *Redstone, Jupiter,* and *Saturn* rockets had fallen back to earth and crashed—or burned on re-entry to the earth's atmosphere—never to be used again. The space shuttle, by contrast, could make many flights, and thus made it easier and cheaper to fly in space.

Engineers at Huntsville applied their knowledge of rockets to building the space shuttle. Throughout the 1970s they perfected the design and performance of the machine that looked like a gigantic airplane. In 1981 the first shuttle, *Columbia,* orbited the earth. Again, there was joy in Huntsville over the achievement. Some of that happiness, however, turned to sadness in January 1986 when the shuttle *Challenger* exploded and burned soon after take-off. Seven astronauts were killed.

The Making of Modern Alabama
by Robert J. Norrell

Left, Jerusalem in miniature at the Ave Maria Grotto in Cullman. Using scrap metal, chewing gum, tinfoil, and bits and pieces of wood and stone he found in the area, Benedictine Brother Joseph Zoettl created more than 125 miniatures of famous churches, shrines, and buildings from around the world.

Overleaf, sailboats docked at the marina in Joe Wheeler State Park.

Peavine Falls at Oak Mountain State Park.

Down at Bluenose's fish trap on the Sipsey River, the water in the big pool above the trap was deep and slow-moving. Then as the river funneled down into the sluiceway, the water picked up speed, pouring through that narrow channel as if driven by some terrific motor hidden on the bottom of the river. Whenever I try to think of the events of those next days, my mind always calls up an image of that run of river, its waters gathering ever faster for the plunge down the narrow chute of the sluiceway. And beyond that chute, the river, like our lives, flowed on but was not the same; its currents sought new channels; the old patterns would not hold.

Whiskey Man
by Howell Raines

CENTRAL ALABAMA

The capitol stands in all its majesty under the summer sun atop Goat Hill in Montgomery, while a few miles away at Jasmine Hill Gardens a replica of Myron's *Discobolus* stands near the exact replica of the ruins of the Temple of Hera and the Olympian Centre with meeting rooms and gift shop.

He hiked over a block to Dexter Avenue, the wide boulevard that ended in front of the capitol. He stood at the bottom of the steps and stared up at the columned front with the clock overhead, all crowned by the silver dome over which flew Old Glory and the Alabama flag with its red corner-to-corner cross on a white background. He sat on the corner of a marble box in which colorful flowers blossomed and he looked back down the eight-lane boulevard and gave silent thanks that he was here.

King of Country
by Wayne Greenhaw

The Governor's Mansion, formerly the Ligon House, built in 1907, on Montgomery's South Perry Street.

Those who love the Old South may take their choice of courses: they may either exist in complacent dreams, hoping that they will not too soon be cast from their beds by a sudden rocking of the earth beneath them; or they may resolve to wrestle with substantial problems with all the strength and skill at their command, inspired by another kind of vision—one which leads them to hope that the present and future of the South may yet prove worthy of the glamorous reputation of the antebellum years.

90 Degrees in the Shade
by Clarence Cason

The Governor's Mansion is not only the home of Alabama's chief executive and family, it is a place where glorious gatherings have been hosted through the years. It is enchanting and graceful, a showplace.

Overleaf, the setting sun floods the sky with color over the Tennessee-Tombigbee Waterway in Demopolis.

Little Tallassee's virgin forests, tilled fields, and broad meadows presented prospects so rich and verdant that they called to mind an exultant passage from Psalms: "The pastures are clothed with flocks; the valleys also are covered with corn; they shout for joy, they also sing."

As we start our horses on a 50-foot bank of the Alabama River—deep enough to float the mighty *Ramillies,* and almost 1,500-feet wide at its headwater—Annalie informed me that this majestic stream flowed generally south and west until it joined the Tombigbee some 40 miles above Mobile, a village and port neither as populous nor as active in trade as Spain's other garrisoned ports of Pensacola to the east and New Orleans to the west.

Alabama Empire
by Welbourn Kelley

Right, this rabbit is a resident of Eufaula National Wildlife Refuge.

Far right, a curious whitetail buck takes a break from grazing in Velvet, near Prattville.

Lifting the Veil of Ignorance, statue at Tuskegee University honoring Booker T. Washington.

I confess that what I saw during my month of travel and investigation (through Alabama) left me with a very heavy heart. The work to be done in order to lift these people up seemed almost beyond accomplishing. I was only one person, and it seemed to me that the little effort I could put forth could go such a short distance toward bringing about results. I wondered if I could accomplish anything, and if it were worthwhile for me to try.

Up From Slavery
by Booker T. Washington

Left, Montgomery folk artist Mose Tolliver (Mose T) is nationally known for his paintings of, among other subjects, whimsical self-portraits, rendered on scrap boards of plywood.

Far left, Montgomery's modern Museum of Fine Arts.

Overleaf, the Carolyn Blount Theatre, home of the Alabama Shakespeare Festival, is a state-of-the-art facility housing two theaters and workshops where plays are developed by the Southern Writers Project.

Page 108, Paul M. Grist State Park, just north of Selma.

When the Montgomery Museum of Fine Arts was founded in 1930 by a group of dedicated citizens and artists, acquisitions were made for the permanent collection with an eye toward the history of the area as well as fine local artists. The group was led by the paintings of J. Kelly Fitzpatrick, one of central Alabama's most highly acclaimed painters . . . Two years before its 60th birthday, the museum opened in its current home within the Wynton M. Blount Cultural Park.

Montgomery: Center Stage in the South
by Wayne Greenhaw and Kathy Holland

Hank Williams wrote about the stars. He may have been thinking of the night the stars fell when he wrote, "The silence of a falling star lights up a purple sky," but it is doubtful. The line is from *I'm So Lonesome I Could Cry,* one of his all-time favorites.

Maybe Hank wrote that song in Montgomery. It was in Montgomery that Hank first put his loneliness, jealousies, fears, disappointments, and dreams to music, peeling back the veneer, and laying bare a troubled heart. His fans loved him for his honesty and his understanding.

Alabama: One Big Front Porch
by Kathryn Tucker Windham

Civil War re-enactments are scattered on battlefields across the state. No major battles were fought in Alabama, but re-enactors uncover every tiny detail about each minor skirmish. They not only dress the part, they use the actual weapons that were used in the mid-nineenth century battles. On horseback or afoot, the re-enactments attempt to make every minute an exact replica of the war of more than a hundred years ago. It is a photographer's dream.

The battle (at Selma) was mercifully short. The three thousand ill-equipped, mostly untrained men spaced out along the horseshoe-shaped defense line were no match for the nine thousand Union soldiers under General Wilson's command, and in less than an hour after the fighting began, the Yankees had breached the lines and were storming the town.

Miraculously, fewer than twenty Confederates were killed in the battle, but among that number was Arthur Small. After the guns were silent and while the city suffered its first agony of pillage and arson, friends lifted the body of the minister from the spot where he had fallen, and they bore him home.

A Sampling of Selma Stories
by Kathryn Tucker Windham

Kirkwood Mansion in Eutaw.

From the orchard across the way, the smell of ripe pears floats over the child's bed. A band rehearses waltzes in the distance. White things gleam in the dark—white flowers and paving-stones. The moon on the window panes careens to the garden and ripples the succulent exhalations of the earth like a silver paddle. The world is younger than it is, and she to herself appears so old and wise, grasping her problems and wrestling with them as affairs peculiar to herself and not as racial heritages. There is a brightness and bloom over things; she inspects life proudly, as if she walked in a garden forced by herself to grow in the least hospitable of soils. She is already contemptuous of ordered planting, believing in the possibility of a wizard cultivator to bring forth sweet-smelling blossoms from the hardest of rocks, and night-blooming vines from barren wastes, to plant the breath of twilight and to shop with marigolds. She wants life to be easy and full of pleasant reminiscences.

Save Me the Waltz
by Zelda Sayre Fitzgerald

"Old times there are not forgotten . . ." The song resounds with a bittersweet sadness, but the nostalgia of yesteryear is illustrated here in the 1920s automobiles and the facades of Wetumpka on the banks of the Coosa River. The movie adapted from Alabama-native Truman Capote's novella, *Grass Harp,* was being made with Walter Mathau and Jack Lemon when Dan Brothers shot this picture of the street scene. The quaint facades remained after Hollywood finished shooting the movie.

116

Left, Chewacla State Park in Auburn.

Opposite, frontier enthusiast Jim Caton of Andalusia participates in a primitive rendezvous in northern Autaga County.

The fiddlers of the Alabama hills have translated the life they and their neighbors live into notes. Fiddle songs are the folk music of their generation, ballads the relic of the past. From the names of these rollicking tunes much of the course of the mountain living may be read. To the uninitiated ear the melodies sound very much alike. There is the same breathless, tumbling pace in all. But the mountaineer dancer can recognize each one by a phrase. He hears in them the cries of the wild beasts in the woods, the creaking of axles, the sounds of work, the crescendo and diminuendo of the express train roaring through the pass.

Stars Fell on Alabama
by Carl Carmer

119

Left, Leonard Bast of Daleville helps re-enact the 1814 construction of Fort Jackson on the Coosa River. Bast is dressed as one of General Andrew Jackson's 2nd Tennessee Volunteers.

Overleaf, the Cahaba River in Bibb County near Centreville.

The spring of 1796 was early, hot, and fairly dry. The Coosa River rolled smooth and full, a fast-flowing stream tinted red-brown by the clay eroded from its banks. It swirled gently around the piles of a long, weather-beaten wharf that lay below the steep, red clay bluff. Casks of tobacco, pork, and untarred rope lay scattered over the worn and splintered planks. Crates of sheet glass leaned against a lumpy pyramid of cotton bales. Twenty sweating Negroes stood in a line from the wharf edge to the tumbled cargo, passing barrels packed with hams down to the waiting flatboats. The river boatmen, whites and halfbreeds, sat or squatted on the wharf, watching the Negroes toil beneath the baking sun.

Horseshoe Bend
by Bruce Palmer and John Clifford Giles

I kept thinking about the words Hosea Williams had said about if you can't vote, then you're a slave. So many black people not only could not vote, but they were even afraid to try to register. I knew that night that being a part of that nonviolent army Dr. King had spoken of was going to be the most important thing in my life. I thought of the stanza in the song "We Shall Overcome" that "God is on our side." With the depth that only a child's mind could feel, I believed those words, believed them dearly.

Selma, Lord, Selma
by Sheyann Webb and
Rachel West Nelson
as told to Frank Sikora

Martin L. King Jr.
Hosea Williams
Ralph Albernathy
Ella Baker
Jesse Jackson
Joseph Lowery
Marie Foster
John Lewis
Fannie L Hamer
Andrew Young
Bernard Lee
Worth Long
Frederick D. Reese
James Bevel
C. T. Vivian
Fred Shuttlesworth
Ceola Miller
Dick Gregory
Albert Turner
James Orange
Annie Cooper
Thurgood Marshall
P. H. Lewis

I HAD
A DREAM

THEY GAVE THEIR LIVES

to overcome injustice
and secure the right
to vote for all Americans

JAMES J. REEB
Boston

VIOLA GREGG LIUZZO
Detroit

JIMMY LEE JACKSON
Marion, Alabama

DR. MARTIN L.
KING JR.

THE DEMONSTRATION THAT LED TO THE MOST IMPOR-
TANT ADVANCE IN CIVIL RIGHTS FOR MILLIONS OF BLACK
AMERICANS BEGAN HERE MARCH 21, 1965. IT WAS THE
50-MILE MARCH FROM SELMA TO MONTGOMERY, ALA-
BAMA, THE STATE CAPITAL.

...UNTIL JUSTICE ROLLS DOWN LIKE WATERS
AND RIGHTEOUSNESS LIKE A MIGHTY STREAM

MARTIN LUTHER KING JR

Left, two young women re-
flect upon the Civil Rights
Memorial in Montgomery.

Far left, Martin Luther King
Memorial at Brown Chapel
AME Church in Selma.

We are now faced with the fact that tomorrow is today. We are confronted with the fierce urgency of *now.* In this unfolding conundrum of life and history there is such a thing as being too late. Procrastination is still the thief of time. Life often leaves us standing bare, naked, and dejected with a lost opportunity. The "tide in the affairs of men" does not remain at the flood; it ebbs. We may cry out desperately for time to pause in her passage, but time is deaf to every plea and rushes on. Over the bleached bones and jumbled residues of numerous civilizations are written the pathetic words: "Too late."

Where Do We Go from Here: Chaos or Community
by Martin Luther King, Jr.

Right, the Montgomery Symphony Orchestra plays on the steps of the Alabama Archives and History building in the capitol complex for an audience gathered for the Montgomery Jubilee. The money to construct this building came mostly from federal funds. The state archivist, Marie Bankhead Owen, traveled to Washington to ask for funds from the Roosevelt administration in the late 1930s since the Depression was virtually over. She asked New Deal leader Harry Hopkins, who dismissed her request immediately. Hopkins told her companion, Alabama Governor Bibb Graves, that the government did not have money "to construct a building for every little old lady wanting an archives." Graves told him that she "was not any little old lady," her brother John was majority leader of the U.S. Senate and her brother William was Speaker of the House of Representatives. After Hopkins realized what he had done, he apologized to Mrs. Owen and asked where in Montgomery she would like the building built.

Overleaf, the Club House at Grand National, Opelika, on the Robert Trent Jones Golf Trail.

128

Creek, Cherokee, Chicasaw, and Choctaw Indians lived in Alabama before the white men came with their guns. Today Native Americans such as Chris Blackburn, left, of the Poarch Band of Creek Indians, celebrate their culture at pow-wows and dances across the state.

Far left, the Cahaba River.

In the quiet Alabama backwater of the Civil War, the Confederate government operated a major prison camp for Union captives. It was at Cahaba, a place formerly of much importance, but also of much adversity. The state's first capital, Cahaba was about ten miles south of Selma at the junction of the Cahaba and Alabama rivers. The prison, on the Alabama's bank, was established in the spring or summer of 1863—the record is inexact. Authorities ordered it closed six to nine months later and sent the captives to the newer and much bigger prison at Andersonville, Georgia. Cahaba Federal Prison, its official name, nevertheless remained a collecting station for men en route to Andersonville and was reestablished as a regular facility when Andersonville overflowed with men and the South became most desperate for everything, including places to keep captured Federal soldiers. Only nine months of war remained when the South made the prison permanent, or as permanent as a dying Confederacy could make anything.

Cahaba Prison and the Sultana Disaster
by William O. Bryant

The solid South stretches away for miles, long clay roads climbing slow hills covered with straggling pines, broad, blank cotton fields, isolated cabins in patches of sand, and far off in the distance the blue promise of hills. The town is lost beside a wide brown swirling river which cuts swiftly under its high red banks on either side. Deep trees overhang the brown foam at the edges, and shadows lie long and sleepily under the Spanish moss where darting hard-shelled insects fall down from the branches. Brown mud oozes between the cobblestones of the ponderous width of Jackson Street where it curls down to the riverside, lined with decaying wharves from the time when there was much shipping on the river.

"Southern Girl"
by Zelda Sayre Fitzgerald

Re-enactors at Fort Toulouse portray 18th-century French Colonial Marines and their belles.

Overleaf, a small craft maneuvers the Alabama River at dusk, Roland Cooper State Park in Camden.

SOUTH ALABAMA

Think of a place in the heart of nowhere. A place made of water, the sky, a salt marsh. Not much else. Trees, a boat. A boy of sixteen with a dangerous imagination.

Later, on one of the last days in May, when the sun was fat red and just inches above the horizon, Victor looked up from his Hardy Boys book and smelled woodsmoke: his grandmother Willie waiting with supper: green beans burned just right in a cast-iron pot, corn bread in the stove, fish lifted from shimmering oil to drain on torn paper bags.

V for Victor
by Mark Childress

Left, netmaker Louie Barber at Nelson's Net Shop, Bayou La Batre.

Opposite, fishing boats at Bayou La Batre.

Overleaf, Perdido River forms part of the Alabama state line. The trees on the right side of the photo are in Baldwin County, those on the left are in Florida.

Pages 142–143, Bragg-Mitchell Mansion in Mobile.

Left, bluff overlooking Tennessee-Tombigbee Waterway in Clarke County.

The wagon jounced under the fingers of trees, a forest of green hands above, shielding the road from the fast-falling sun. The stillness gave way to the creak of the wheels and the mare's easy rhythm. Stella cushioned her mother's head in her lap, hearing his words again, like a song in her head: Go home now, go home, just drive gentle and slow, just take care that you drive just as slow as you can, and be sweet when she wakes, use these pills for the pain, now that poor child is gone and it's nobody's fault. I'll be out . . .

They passed through a region of gray stunted trees, with tops broken off by some old vicious wind. They rounded the bend by the Gibsons' small house, starting up the slow red rise to their own. As the wheels dunked in the creek, Callie awoke with a soft startled cry. Stella nestled her close, her thighs numb with the sight, and bent low to speak. "It's all right, Mama, we near home now." She leaned back. "William! Slow up. She's awake."

A World Made of Fire
by Mark Childress

145

In downtown Enterprise in 1919, when a passerby asked, "Hey, what are y'all doing?" a workman replied jokingly, "We're putting up a big statue honoring the boll weevil." Then he went back to work and never even thought about his flippant reply again.

It happened that a stranger passing along the sidewalk heard the remark. He had no idea the workman was joking, so when he was in Montgomery the next day he called the *Advertiser* and told a reporter that Enterprise was building a monument to the boll weevil.

The reporter recognized a good story when he heard one, and he didn't want to run the risk of spoiling it by investigating it too closely. He wrote the story just the way he heard it.

When the citizens of Enterprise read in the *Advertiser* that they were building a monument to the boll weevil, they were surprised as everything. They recognized a good story, too, and made a quick decision to do what the newspaper story said they were doing.

They've never been sorry.

Alabama: One Big Front Porch
by Kathryn Tucker Windham

Right, "They look almost real," visitors say about the soldiers climbing from the helicopter at the U.S. Army Aviation Museum at Fort Rucker near Ozark.

Opposite, Enterprise's boll weevil monument.

Overleaf, Byrnes Lake, Mobile Delta.

146

Bellingrath Gardens near Mobile is always beautiful, whether with the shades of reds and pinks of azaleas in early spring or the full-bloomed flowers of summer. This colorful photo was taken in November.

150

Bellingrath Gardens is one of those places that makes you feel better about the way the Great American Fortunes have been spent. When Coca-Cola first came on the market in 1903, the Bellingraths took over the bottling franchise for the state. Being people of simple tastes, she inclined to garden and he to fishing. When they got a little spare cash in 1917 they bought some land on the Isle-des-Olies (Isle of Geese) below Mobile to set up a fishing camp. The result is 800 acres of horticultural perfection which has been open to the public 365 days a year since 1932.

An Alabama Journal
by Scottie Fitzgerald Smith

In August, 1864, Admiral David Farragut won the battle of Mobile Bay, capturing Forts Gaines and Morgan, thus gaining control of the lower bay. However, for almost a year the Union forces were unable to break through the land defenses that guarded the city of Mobile.

Fort Blakeley was not a typical fortification but was a four-mile-long barricade of pine logs covered with sand and mud, and was constructed with nine luettes, or zig-zags, in the line. The flanks rested on the marshes of the Appalachee River. There were 2,700 Confederate soldiers behind these lines or in advanced rifle pits, and 35 pieces of artillery plus siege mortars, which made the position more formidable than nearby Spanish Fort. The Confederate commander was General St. John Liddle, a West Pointer and veteran of the Tennessee campaigns.

Ordered to capture Mobile, Union General E. R. S. Camby led 32,000 men from Forts Gaines and Morgan on March 17, 1865, while Union Major-General Frederick Steele moved northwestward from Pensacola with 13,000 troops. The two columns converged on Spanish Fort, where the defenders held out against the vastly superior numbers for sixteen days.

On April 1, the forces under Steele arrived before Fort Blakely with 75 wagon-loads of supplies and immediately began a bombardment of the Confederate fort from only 1,000 yards away, which lasted until April 8, accompanied by infantry skirmishes, sniper fire, and the roar of small arms fire.

On April 8, Canby secured Spanish Fort and immediately began to shift his men northward for three miles to join Steele before Fort Blakeley. By late afternoon 22,000 Union soldiers had massed for an attack. At 5 p.m., the Union brigades rushed toward the center of the Confederate line, breaking through the shattered abatis by the sheer power of numbers. Some of the defenders were able to escape into the marshes, but 2,300 surrendered to Union forces.

Dead Towns of Alabama
by W. Stuart Harris

Stories are told about this spot at the end of the peninsula that points westward at the mouth of Mobile Bay. Here Fort Morgan guarded the waters to keep enemy ships from entering and attacking the port city of Mobile. It was in these waters that Union Admiral David C. Farragut went against Confederate battleship *Tennessee* and the forty guns of Fort Morgan on the morning of August 5, 1864.

Left, fishing wharf at Bon Secour.

Overleaf, Lake Jackson at Florala State Park.

Here was one of the most beautiful places Peter had ever seen. A triangle of sandy beach pointed into the bay, and on the point of the triangle was one lonely battered cypress tree. Coming out of the underbrush behind and flowing through the roots of the tree was a perfectly clear creek overlaced by limbs trailing garlands of moss and vines. Back the way they had come, the high clay cliff had grown once more into perspective, and the wharves they had passed were diminutive now. Ahead, the land pointed off again, and houses broke but did not disturb the landscape. Their wharves were closer and reflected in the water, wavering across the distance.

The Butterfly Tree
by Robert Bell

Once Goodtown, or Goodtown Bay, had pelicans, brown pelicans, by the dozens, great ragged-winged, ungainly, buoyant, bent-necked, long-beaked foolish bags of feathers gliding along at the wavetops like balloons with wings, or hunched motionless in solitary, precarious-seeming balance on the tops of pilings, like old forgotten, sculptured bogies left behind—oh, long ago—to mock the gods of sun and sea at the earth's edge, pelicans that now, in all their foolishness and grandeur, were, Claude pointed out, damn well, and that was the hell of it, gone.

A Bird in the Hand
by Donald Wetzel

Mobile has the oldest Mardi Gras of all the pre-Lenten festivals in the United States. Thousands of people line Government Street downtown, where the parades of the participants wind during the morning, noon, and night of the celebration period, ending with the largest and longest on Fat Tuesday, followed by a masked ball. The costumes are colorful and unique, following the customs of one of the state's most traditional cities.

Right, the *USS Ala-bama,* docked in Mobile Bay just east of downtown Mobile.

Overleaf, Bayou La Batre.

During the early 1830s, large ocean-going ships were barred from sailing to the port of Mobile by a large sandbar extending from the mouth of Dog River, and businessmen found it expensive to transfer cargoes to light draught boats, therefore Alabama City was founded as a port on the other side of the bay. The town first appeared on a state map in 1838, located on the Bay Shore Road, between the towns of Blakeley and Williamsburg. For a short time it posed a threat to the commerce of Mobile, but became unimportant when the panic of 1837 ruined its principal backers. It continued to be on state maps until the early 1880s, but had disappeared in 1895 when Fairhope was established on the site.

Dead Towns of Alabama
by W. Stuart Harris

166

Left, secondary sand dunes on Dauphin Island.

Overleaf, Fairhope Municipal Pier, on the eastern shore of Mobile Bay.

The pier at Fairhope was a plank promenade running straight out from the foot of Bay Street for two hundred yards over shallow water—waiting, at all hours, for anyone who cared to pick out a path across the uneven boards, being mindful of fishhooks and invisible gaps which could cause you to fall and spill your bait. On hot nights like this, there was always somebody. People fled their kitchens and rooms to come and sit in the dark over the bay, where a breeze might get at them and where, if they dangled a chicken drumstick at the end of a string, they might catch a blue crab for the gumbo.

V for Victor
by Mark Childress

171

The Robert Trent Jones Golf Trail, comprising seven courses spread across the state, offers a variety and level of public golf unmatched anywhere in the world. Six of the seven courses can be found in *Golf Digest*'s list of America's Top 75 Affordable Courses, and two rank among the top 10. All the courses were designed by Robert Trent Jones, Sr., arguably the premier golf course architect in the world, and represent the culmination of his unparalleled career. At right is the Cambrian Ridge course in Greenville, ranked No. 13.

174

Annual Blessing of the Fleet,
Bayou La Batre.

Alabama felt a magic descending, spreading, long ago. Since then it has been a land with a spell on it—not a good spell, always. Moons, red with the dust of barren hills, thin pine trunks barring horizons, festering swamps, restless yellow rivers, are all part of a feeling—a strange certainty that above and around them hovers enchantment—an emanation of malevolence that threatens to destroy men through dark ways of its own. It is difficult to translate this feeling into words, yet almost every visitor to this land has known it and felt in some degree what I felt with increasing wonder during the six years I lived there . . .

Those who really know, the black conjure women in their weathered cabins along the Tombigbee, tell a . . . story. They say that on the memories of the oldest slaves their fathers knew there was one indelible imprint of an awful event—a shower of stars over Alabama. Many an Alabamian to this day reckons dates from "the year the stars fell"—though he and his neighbor frequently disagree as to what year of our Lord may be so designated. All are sure, however, that once upon a time stars fell on Alabama, changing the land's destiny. What had been written in eternal symbols was thus erased—and the region has existed ever since, unreal and fated, bound by a horoscope such as controls no other country.

Stars Fell on Alabama
by Carl Carmer

Above, winners of the 1993 Dauphin Island Regatta, catamaran division, crossing the finish line.

Left, Gulf State Park fishing pier.

Above, the multi-colored murals painted on the walls of downtown buildings in Dothan, the centerpiece of the Wiregrass in southeast Alabama, tell the history of the state. The city commissioned the artwork to celebrate its long and colorful history as well as to make the exterior walls of the town an outdoor museum.

On the right, the underground passageway leads to Fort Morgan, and over it fly the seven flags which have flown over Alabama during its history: from the state flag on the far left, the flag of the Confederate states, French, U.S., Alabama territory, British, and Spanish.

A cannon at Fort Gaines, used in the Battle of Mobile Bay.

Right, Alabama Point near Gulf Shores is a favorite vacation place for many, whether to enjoy the deep-sea fishing, swimming in the crystal-clear water, eating the seafood from shrimp to grouper to mullet, or just lazing in the noonday sun.

Overleaf: sunrise at Alabama Point.

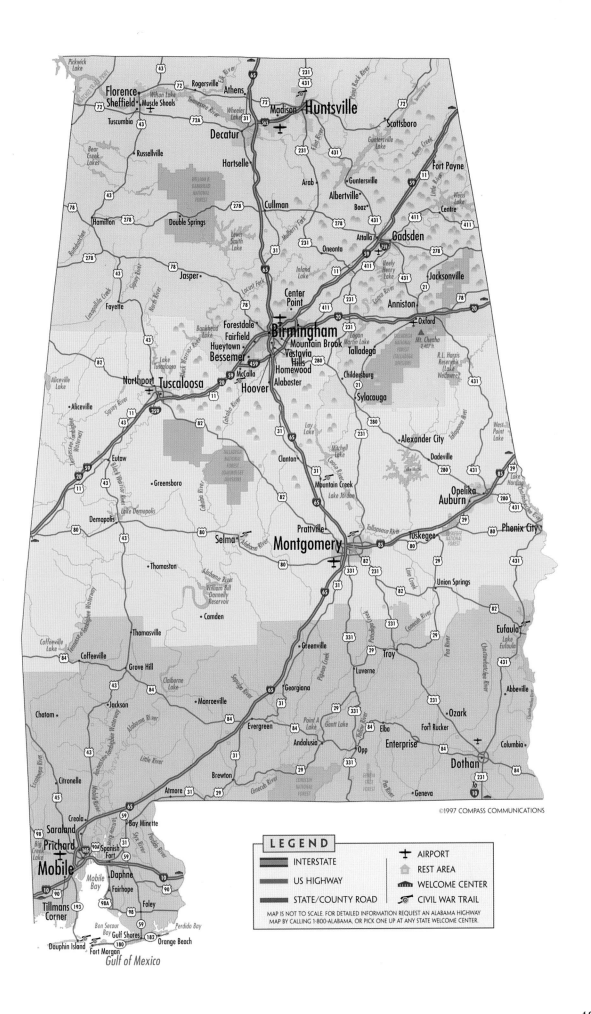

LEGEND

INTERSTATE
US HIGHWAY
STATE/COUNTY ROAD

AIRPORT
REST AREA
WELCOME CENTER
CIVIL WAR TRAIL

MAP IS NOT TO SCALE. FOR DETAILED INFORMATION REQUEST AN ALABAMA HIGHWAY
MAP BY CALLING 1-800-ALABAMA, OR PICK ONE UP AT ANY STATE WELCOME CENTER.

©1997 COMPASS COMMUNICATIONS

Bibliography

Abernethy, Thomas Perkins. *The Formative Period in Alabama, 1815-1828,* The University of Alabama Press, Tuscaloosa, Alabama, 1990.

Barnard, William D. *Dixiecrats and Democrats: Alabama Politics, 1942-1950,* The University of Alabama Press, Tuscaloosa, Alabama, 1974.

Blue, M.P. *A Brief History of Montgomery,* T.C. Bingham and Company, Montgomery, 1878.

Brantley, William H., Jr. *Three Capitals: St. Stephens, Huntsville & Cahawba, 1818-1826,* The University of Alabama Press, Tuscaloosa, Alabama, 1976.

Bordin, Ruth: *Woman and Temperance: The Quest for Power and Liberty, 1873-1900,* Temple University Press, Philadelphia, Pennsylvania, 1981.

Brown, Jerry Elijah, editor. *Clearings in the Thicket: An Alabama Humanities Reader,* Mercer University Press, Macon, Georgia, 1983.

Brown, Jerry Elijah, and Henry DeLeon Southerland, Jr. *The Federal Road,* The University of Alabama Press, Tuscaloosa, Alabama, 1989.

DuBose, John Witherspoon. *The Life and Times of William Lowndes Yancey,* Volumes I and II, Peter Smith, New York, 1942.

Flynt, Wayne. *Montgomery: An Illustrated History,* Windsor Publications Inc., Woodland Hills, California, 1980.

Gamble, Robert. *Historic Architecture in Alabama: A Primer of Styles and Types, 1810-1930,* The University of Alabama Press, Tuscaloosa, Alabama, 1990.

Gamble, Robert. *The Alabama Catalog: A Guide to the Early Architecture of the State,* The University of Alabama Press, Tuscaloosa, Alabama, 1987.

Going, Allen Johnston. *Bourbon Democracy in Alabama, 1874-1890,* The University of Alabama Press, Tuscaloosa, Alabama, 1992.

Gosse, Philip Henry. *Letters from Alabama,* The University of Alabama Press, Tuscaloosa, Alabama, 1993, introduction by Henry H. Jackson III.

Greenhaw, Wayne. *Elephants in the Cottonfields: Ronald Reagan and the New Republican South,* Macmillan, New York, 1981.

Greenhaw, Wayne. *Montgomery: The Biography of a City,* The Advertiser Company, Montgomery, Alabama, 1993.

Jordan, Wymouth T. *Ante-Bellum Alabama: Town and Country,* The University of Alabama Press, Tuscaloosa, Alabama, 1987.

O'Donnell, Joe. *Birmingham: Magic City Renaissance,* Community Communications, Montgomery, Alabama, 1992.

Parks, Rosa, with Jim Haskins. *Rosa Parks: My Story,* Dial Books, New York, 1992.

Pickett, Albert James: *History of Alabama and Incidentally of Georgia and Mississippi,* Birmingham Book and Magazine Company, Birmingham, Alabama, 1962, originally published in 1851 and 1878.

Rogers, William Warren, Robert David Ward, Leah Rawls Atkins, and Wayne Flynt. *Alabama: The History of a Deep South State,* The University of Alabama Press, Tuscaloosa, Alabama, 1994.

Stewart, John Craig. *Governors of Alabama,* Pelican Publishing Company, Gretna, Louisiana, 1975.

Strode, Hudson. *Jefferson Davis: Confederate President,* Harcourt Brace & World, New York, 1959.

Sulzby, James F., Jr. *Historic Alabama Hotels and Resorts,* The University of Alabama Press, Tuscaloosa, Alabama, 1960.

Thomas, Mary Martha. *The New Woman in Alabama: Social Reforms and Suffrage: 1890-1920,* The University of Alabama Press, Tuscaloosa, Alabama, 1992.

Williams, Clanton Ware. *The Early History of Montgomery and Incidentially of The State of Alabama,* Confederate Publishing Company, University, Alabama, 1979, edited with introduction by W. Stanley Hoole and Addie S. Hoole.